7/19

VINTAGE NELL

∞ ∞

The McCafferty Reader

Editor Elgy Gillespie spent much of the seventies
sharing a desk with Nell McCafferty and six mes-
senger boys in *The Irish Times* newsroom while
Nell was writing 'In the Eyes of the Law'. In the
late eighties she left to edit the *San Francisco
Review of Books*. She is author of *The Liberties of
Dublin* (1974) and numerous reference works that
include *The Rough Guide to San Francisco Restaurants* (2004). She edited *Changing the Times:
Irish Women Journalists 1969-1981* (2003) for
Lilliput and writes for the San Francisco website
Travelocity, while teaching Vocational English to
immigrant Latino and Asian workers.

PREVIOUS BOOKS BY NELL McCAFFERTY

The Best of Nell, Attic Press 1984, 1993, 2005
Goodnight Sisters, Attic Press 1987
In the Eyes of the Law, Ward River Press 1981
Peggy Deery
A Woman to Blame: The Kerry Babies Case
Armagh Women
Nell, Penguin Books, 2004 and 2005 (pbk)

VINTAGE NELL

The McCafferty Reader

edited by Elgy Gillespie

The Lilliput Press Dublin

ACKNOWLEDGMENTS

Heartfelt thanks to Irene Stevenson with Esther
Murnane at *The Irish Times*' library; to Cambridge
University Library's Ann Toseland; to Dermot
Carroll and the Dublin City Library; and San
Francisco copyeditors Anne Kirwan and Sarah
Champion; also to Michael McLoughlin at Pen-
guin Books for permission to use 'Lily'.

PRODUCTION/LAYOUT EDITOR CATHERINE BARRY

A Dubliner born and bred, Catherine Barry has
worked in publishing in areas of editorial, photo-
graphy and design for twenty years. She has
worked and lived in Ireland, England and Aus-
tralia, and now lives in San Francisco with her
nine-year old son David.

First published 2005 by
THE LILLIPUT PRESS
62–63 Sitric Road, Arbour Hill
Dublin 7, Ireland
www.lilliputpress.ie

Copyright © Nell McCafferty, 2005

ISBN 1 84351 068 5

1 3 5 7 9 10 8 6 4 2

Set in 12 pt on 14 pt Times New Roman
Printed in England by MPG Books, Cornwall

CONTENTS

PREFACE

NELL McCAFFERTY

When I began journalism in 1970, there was a war in the North of Ireland, the root cause of which was the definition of that place as a Protestant state for a Protestant people, to which the ruling British government turned a blind eye. That war is over now, as is the one-party statelet, and the principle of a power-sharing government has been agreed. The IRA decommissioned its arsenal in September 2005, ending eight hundred years of armed struggle against Britain.

In 1970 the South was a mirror image of the North: a Catholic state for a Catholic people, actively encouraged by the Irish government. Thanks mainly to the war fought against patriarchy by feminists on the battleground of control of women's bodies, the South is now governed by secular principles instead of religious.

In 2005 North and South are moving slowly together as one people on one island. This collection of articles is about what it felt like from 1970 onwards to live in both parts of Ireland. Sometimes it felt rotten—in the North you got shot at, in the South you got condemned.

Women were always at the bottom of both heaps. Male rulers felt that this was the natural order of things. Indeed, Irish Tánaiste and Minister for Finance, George Colley, was moved to warn females that members of the Irish women's Liberation Movement were both 'well-heeled and articulate'. He thought that was a bad thing for women to aspire to be. He was speaking after the feminists had imported birth control pills into the Republic, where possession of contraceptives was a criminal offence punishable by penal servitude.

If things were awful North and South, the fight to change the status quo was hugely enjoyable. It was my privilege as a journalist to meet the people who brought about change in their homes and towns and villages.

Sometimes I was censored or banned for what I wrote and broadcast. Still, we won, sisters and brothers. We changed our world for the better.

September 2005

FOREWORD

∞ ∞

MARGARET MAC CURTAIN

Nell McCafferty is unequalled in the extraordinary breadth and fearless candour she has brought to bear on controversial subjects we all needed to know about, to which she brought meaning and readability.

Let me give you a little flavour of her home place. In the tiny area of the Bogside where Nell was born, in the house that is still her home, lived or were born John Hume of the SDLP, Martin McGuinness and Mitchell McLoughlin of Sinn Féin, Councillor Mary Nelis, poet Seamus Deane, brilliant debater Eamonn McCann, Paddy Doherty of the Inner City Trust, peacemaker Brendan Duddy, and Nell herself. Nor is Nell ungenerous towards Rosemary Brown from the High Flats, who won the Eurovision for Ireland as Dana in 1970, and is still a very vocal presence in Ireland.

After Nell entered the sixties, she enrolled in Queen's University Belfast as an Arts undergraduate, leaving behind a richly textured childhood and her family at Number 8 Beechwood Street, as well as the friendly neighbourhood to which she returned all her life where crime was negligible. Above them rose the walls surrounding the town centre and the Unionist stronghold, while everything outside the walls comprised the Bogside where the Catholics lived. There was the beach in Buncrana for summer swimming and family walks across the Border on Sunday mornings for

9

cheaper food in the Donegal shops. Though she had serious illnesses as a child between the ages of six and ten, Nell made it effortlessly into Thornhill Grammar School, an all-girls convent school, and from there won a grant to Queen's.

The most real people to her at Queen's were not her teachers, nor the distinguished speakers that came to the English Lit. society of which she was secretary, but her contemporaries: Eamonn McCann, Austin Currie and John Taylor, while two years ahead of her were Deane, Hume and the songwriter Phil Coulter—all from Derry, and all household names in the decades to come, including herself.

Bernadette McAliskey, then Devlin, was to join that list and, much later, President Mary McAleese. When it comes to destiny, they were the first to embrace the future knowingly, and with desperate resolve. Between them all they created a radical new template for the political land-scape of Ireland. Was it free education that made them exceptional, or was it the rising expectation of revolution that Marxist analysis offered, and which may have applied at home in Derry in the late sixties? There are still so many questions we continue to ask of this decade, for which Nell's personal experiences inform our tentative answers. She compels us to recognize that we are far from revising or romanticizing that time.

From the time Donal Foley hired her in 1969, and gave her carte blanche to write up court cases in *The Irish Times* under the title 'In the Eyes of the Law' she has given us riv-eting vignettes—not just of the unsavoury sides of Irish life, but necessary wake-up calls about what was happening in situations where we desperately needed to be enlight-ened. Her piece 'Consenting Adults' offered a bleak com-ment on the humiliations of the early seventies before Mary Robinson and David Norris took up the cudgels on behalf of gay rights. She was called to Washington with a group of prestigious people from Northern Ireland that included

Bishop Ned Daly of Derry, a family friend, and invited to testify before the House of Representatives Committee on Foreign Affairs.

In 1980 her piece about the Armagh Women was published in *The Irish Times*, and women prisoners became an agonizing reality with the opening sentence of what the 'dirty protest' entailed. There was her coverage of the Kerry Babies inquiry for the *Irish Press*, later collected as *A Woman to Blame*, and *Peggy Deery, An Irish Family at War*, both published by Attic Press. Nell always published with small Irish publishers and Attic Press issued two more collections of her writing, *The Best of Nell* in 1984 and *Goodnight Sisters* in 1986.

She was awarded Best Journalist of the Year by *Hibernia* early in her writing career, and in 1990 she received a Golden Globe award for her coverage of the World Cup soccer summer in Italy. Staffordshire University gave her an honorary doctorate alongside Mo Mowlam. Together with Saint Brigid, Grainuaile and Mary Robinson, she is one of the most cited references in *The Field Day Anthology of Irish Writing*, and four of her essays appear in different sections of Field Day's fifth volume: 'Caoineadh Mná na hÉireann' about the abortion debate, and 'The Death of Ann Lovett,' from *In Dublin*. From *Magill* came 'The Peace People at War' in 1980, and the witty and satirical 'Golden Balls'. Her *Sunday Tribune* and *Hot Press* articles from the late 1990s are republished here for the first time; as she approached her sixtieth birthday in 2004, Penguin Books gave us her autobiography, *Nell*, to which the moving Afterword, 'Lily', written about her mother's death that December, appeared in the 2005 paperback edition, and concludes this anthology.

Poet Adrienne Rich has a phrase that illustrates Nell's work: 'To unlearn not to speak' was the task that women's liberationists applied to themselves and that June Levine and Nell describe so vividly in their accounts. Their efforts culminated in the episode of the Contraceptive Train from Belfast to Dublin on 22 May 1971, and the subsequent appearance of the lawbreakers on Irish television's *Late Late Show* that night.

Nell has been teaching women ever since to unlearn the habit of holding their tongues—not easy for Irish women. Nell never flinched from verbal confrontation, and provided lessons in moral courage and truthfulness that many of us took to heart. In *Nell* she admits her fear of death as she cowered beside Burntollet Bridge, and her longing for the safety of home when caught in the panic of Bloody Sunday. Much later, she experienced the same feeling of panic when she covered the Siege of Sarajevo for the Dublin papers.

Hilda Tweedy remembers Nell's activities in the early years of the Council for the Status of Women, which she chaired. In 1975 the Council hosted a series of events to mark the inauguration of International Women's Year. Said Hilda, 'Nell was unstoppable those years, she fearlessly protested against and exposed the government's delay in implementing the EEC directive requiring member states to eliminate all discrimination on grounds of sex in the work-place. Equal pay was a burning issue.'

On the occasion of a state reception hosted by the then Minister for Labour in the National Gallery, Hilda Tweedy and several UN dignitaries were blocked by protesters in their limousine. After some delay, Nell's curly head appeared through the open window beside the driver and Nell addressed Mrs Tweedy: 'Hilda, we have no quarrel with you or your guests, it's that so-and-so waiting to shake hands with you we want to rattle!'

One valuable insight I gained from Nell's reflections and the feeling of defeat that many women experienced during the eighties was that, despite the divisiveness of the

Pro-Life campaign for the Amendment, Irishwomen actually understood the meaning of sisterhood. Perhaps they understood it in the deepest sense, since women shared the hardships of imprisonment in Kilmainham during the civil war of 1922-3. This was palpable as the presidential election of 1990 loomed. I found that section of her book engrossing, and it brought back to me the fundraising, the way we tiptoed around feminist confrontational issues, the people we lobbied—and then the astounding consolation prize, the election of Mary Robinson after the woes of that decade.

With *Nell*, she chose to write an autobiography rather than a memoir—a chronology that moves the narrative along. Anyone looking for Nell at her most candid and most passionate will find her in her revealing account of the transforming relationship with another woman writer where she runs the gamut of honesty, true love, anger, loneliness, peevishness, desolation—all sorts of emotions .

It was a 'first' in Irish female autobiographical writing. What Fintan O'Toole remarked in *The Irish Times* about Nell's critical writing holds true here too, that she radically broke new ground in Ireland. In a *Sunday Tribune* interview Anne-Marie Hourihan suggested that the great romance in Nell's life had been her mother, and Nell did not dismiss the idea. Kathy Sheridan in *The Irish Times* also explored the mother-daughter theme .

But for me, the passion of Nell's life has been Derry and its people, particularly her Bogside neighbours. She shared her grief with her readers as she read down the list of 3,630 people named as killed in *Lost Lives*, and she mourned for the remarkable place that is Derry City even as she enfolds it in her embrace.

With this new Lilliput Press collection of *Vintage Nell*, we congratulate her on a lifetime of journalism and of informed non-fiction, and we hope she will continue to enrich us with her critical thoughts on social issues. More than anything else we want for her the enjoyment of the writing she wishes to pursue for the rest of her life, and that she will achieve her expressed aim: 'I will write until I die.'

Margaret Mac Curtain, also known as Sister Benvenuta, is an historian and member of the Dominican Sisters of Blackrock, Co. Dublin.

NUMBER SEVEN

∞∞∞∞∞∞∞∞∞∞∞∞∞∞∞∞∞∞∞∞∞∞∞∞

THE IRISH TIMES
JANUARY 1970

An American journalist, writing for a newspaper in California, described Number 7 Wellington Street as 'a humble shack in the Bogside.' Dermie and his mother Mrs McClenaghan lived there until last Thursday night. Dermie is twenty-eight, an ex-dental mechanic turned accounts clerk. Since he left school he has always been on one committee or another—Legion of Mary, Boys Club, Labour Party, North-West Council of Social Services, Derry Citizens Action Committee—but he has never figured in the headlines. He is the boy with the beard from the Bogside.

The Californian was one of one hundred and twenty-seven journalists, photographers and TV crews who had to call at Dermie's house during the August riots for a security pass, in the shape of an armband bearing the wearer's name and number. An Egyptian journalist walked the Bogside for three days with 'Winker 98' printed on his armband courtesy of Dermie, who would not embarrass the fellow by asking him to repeat his unpronounceable name in his broken English.

Number 7 Wellington Street comprised two bedrooms, a sitting room, a kitchen, a scullery and an outside toilet. Dermie's father once partitioned the scullery and installed a bath but the result was so cramped, Dermie said, that 'you stepped out of the bath into the cooker.' So they knocked down the partition and sold the bath to an enterprising farmer as a sheep dip. Like all houses in the Bogside, the rooms had a strategic use. If you were of unknown origin you were shown into the sitting room. When you entered the family circle you graduated to the kitchen. And when you were part of the furniture you went out to the scullery and buttered your own bread.

None of the doors ever closed properly. The kitchen door was secured by wedging a towel in it. To the uninitiated it must have seemed like a secret society. I remember one man to whom I handed the towel as he entered going out to the scullery and ceremoniously washing and drying his hands while we sat shivering in the draught.

Number 7 was a meeting place for the world and his wife. Mrs McClenaghan never asked you any questions. She met you at the door and said, 'Aye, Dermie's in, come on in surely,' and then retired to the scullery to make tea, and sometimes in the aftermath when she was emptying ashtrays, she would hope we weren't communists. Dr Abernethy, Governor of the Apprentice Boys, called there regularly to discuss horses with Dermie's cattle-drover father.

Years ago, Ivan Cooper borrowed Mrs McClenaghan's kitchen table and four chairs to use on a continental camping holiday and he and Dermie sold them in Paris for petrol. The Labour Party held its first meeting there around the same kitchen table and planned a housing march to Belfast that was later called off because of foot-and-mouth disease. A decision to defy the 5 October march was taken there.

Conor Cruise O'Brien, up from Dublin on a post-riot tour, was directed to Number 7 as 'Bogside Headquarters.' An enthusiastic Fianna Fáil minister gave Eamonn McCann fifty pounds as they stood in the scullery to use for 'propaganda purposes' after Taoiseach Jack Lynch's broadcast— and Eamonn produced a classic 'Barricades Bulletin' carrying a front-page attack on the southern government. The famous photograph of Radio Free Derry's 'secret head-quarters' brought a furious letter from Dermie's sister, married to a Free State garda, who recognized the picture of the Sacred Heart above the transmitter. The Dubliners gave a concert in the sitting room one Sunday morning and Ciaran kissed Mrs McClenaghan—but as Dermie later remarked, 'Frank Sinatra's never called.'

Number 7 was closed down on Thursday night courtesy of the Northern Ireland Housing Trust slum clearance scheme, and Brendan Hinds unscrewed the number off the door to give to Bernadette Devlin as a memento of her stay there. The removal was a short one across the street to a totally new environment—Glenfadda Park. The holy pictures were installed first with a wry comment from Dermie: 'When the saints go marching in.' The new address is somehow ludicrous, there being not one blade of grass in the concrete courtyard around which the flats are built. Dermie said they were moving out of little boxes into a filing cabinet. All the doors to the flats are closed and the place is curiously quiet. There is no street to scuffle your feet on or look up and down to 'see what's new.' You can't sit on the front windowsill and talk to the boys since there is a thirty-foot drop to the ground below. But in terms of comparative physical comfort the new house is a joy.

You can see it in little things—sugar bowl and milk jugs and bread slices on a plate. Formerly these things were kept in their original containers because sugar standing overnight in a bowl in a damp house becomes lumpy, and bread outside the wax wrapping paper becomes hard. In the spacious living room, you no longer have to eat in shifts if there are more than three people for a meal. In Wellington Street, the drop-leaf table always stayed folded because if you extended it properly someone would be sitting in the fireplace and Mrs McClenaghan couldn't get in the door

17

with the teapot. The new long living room seems vast by comparison. If you sit at the far end and watch television, Mrs McClenaghan says it's like going to the pictures. She wants a loud hailer for when she 'calls Dermie for his tea'.

The bathroom always evokes delight. The facecloth doesn't have tea leaves and the soap doesn't smell of onions. You don't have to boil a kettle in the morning for hot water to wash your face, and despair if you put too much cold water in the basin afterwards. Now Dermie turns on hot and cold taps and whistles until the temperature of the water is just so.

Mrs McClenaghan bought a magnificent new carpet for the living room and doesn't have to worry about rot seeping up from the damp floors under it. And if she still insists on covering it with the *Derry Journal* to protect it from muddy feet, it is only until the Commission has fixed up the new road outside.

A DAY I SPENT WITH PAISLEY

THE IRISH TIMES
APRIL 1970

Alone in Crumlin Road Courthouse in Belfast at 9 am on Tuesday morning, Ian Paisley doggedly began his working day as he had thunderously begun his crowded open air meeting the previous night—in pursuit of law and order. He laid the complaints before the returning officer that a woman had been driving around the Bannside, stealing his postal votes.

He then spent an hour in the offices of the Puritan Printing Company Limited with his youthful election agent, the Reverend Beggs, a charming clerical version of Anthony Perkins. At 11 am he appeared in the village of Ahoghill, Bannside. His local contact man scuttled ahead of him, knocking on doors, pointing back to the big man. Scrubbed and smiling, solid in the drizzling rain, Paisley moves steadily from house to house, forthrightly introducing himself as a Protestant Unionist candidate. 'And here's some literature for you!'

He filled the doorway, hands on either side of it, leaning in, looking down, the brief seconds large with his presence. I asked a woman why she was voting for him, and she was astonished at my ignorance: 'The Lord's Word must be spread.' What did she want from him politically?

'Material things don't matter when we're before our Maker.' In slum dwellings of the main street, the occupants seize him with delight. 'Thon Minford never came this far

19

yesterday. You speak up for us, Doctor Paisley.'

At 1 pm, the village covered, Paisley stepped into his car and drove off. A covered jeep, little Union Jacks on the bonnet and Scots céilí music coming lightly from the amplifier followed, with me and my taxi behind. We lost them at a country crossroads. Later we found the parked jeep and Wesley the puzzled driver beside it. A petrol pump owner from Lisburn, he didn't know the area. 'You couldn't keep up with the Reverend. I never seen such a busy man.'

He talks matter of factly to me about the fires of hell. He had been saved from the paths of darkness five years ago. 'And I attend the Doctor's church three times a week now. He's a real man of God.'

We decided to go to Ballymena to election headquarters, where Paisley himself answered the door, a sandwich stuck in his mouth. 'Come on in Wesley, we've only a couple of minutes.' I stood damply behind, dying for a cup of tea, and he closed the door in my face. My taxi driver went away for lunch and never came back. I felt like a lonely little Republican. Wesley came out and invited me to sit in the jeep. He was very friendly and said I could travel around in the jeep with him. Paisley arrived and decided not to use the car as he was going into farming country. He unsmilingly told me that to be honest he would rather I get myself other transport.

Wesley blushed. I stood on the street as I remembered the services I had attended at the Doctor's church on Ravenhill Road. An amazingly personal and personable man, Ian Paisley preached an impersonal sermon: 'Salvation is between Christ and you. It will not come through the Roman Church or the Protestant Church or my Church. Salvation comes through Jesus and the Bible.'

From the austerity of the Lord's Word we were drawn quickly back to the intimacy of the pulpit politician on the Ulster scene. He leaned forward, grinning, arms on the pulpit, as the country's leaders are lashed, dismissed and belittled with a joke. The eyes close, the head is bowed, and then up again to Christ Crucified. We sing tunefully of Jesus, accompanied by an organ, and the man beside me smiles widely, eyes bright, singing to the Saviour. He gives me a Polo mint. The basket is passed, filled gladly with money, and then it's time to be saved. Some people go to the front of the church returning to the Lord, and then pass on to a back room where Dr Paisley will later talk to them.

*   *   *

The service over, the organ pumps us out; many remain behind, lingering in the aisles or in the benches, chatting in groups, hovering near the inner rooms where the Doctor receives his parishioners. He moves quickly to and fro, talking, laughing, giving directions. A boy is going to London to look for a job and Paisley gives him the address of a colleague there. Then he says, 'Wait a minute,' rings up the colleague and tells him to expect the boy off the boat train tomorrow evening. He shakes the boy's hand, 'God bless you son, drop us a line, goodbye.' Then he puts his arm around a young couple who want to get married. He sweeps them into his office, joking about their impatience. He's a big man with a big voice, but he leans quietly over an old woman in the corner, chatting to her while we stand around waiting to get a word with him, a smile from him, and we agree that he is a good man of God.

It is 10 pm, ninety minutes after the end of the service, but people are still in the church and Mrs Paisley and her children move amongst them. Paisley is in his office on the phone discussing Election Day caravans with his brother-in-law and men are queuing up to sign on as election workers and to offer cars.

I caught up with Dr Paisley in Cloughmills, a quiet

country village. The men in the pubs say they are not going to vote. 'We're all right here, without them cowboys from Belfast, they never came down here before except that noo they're afeared. Thon Minford can't talk.'

They chuckle when I ask about Paisley. 'He won't be coming in here for a drink.' What do they think of McHugh? They thought it's a pity about him. They talked about the moon shot and Leeds United.

Paisley was going the rounds of the doors, apologizing for interrupting at suppertime. He spoke to a worried woman whose mother lived alone in Grace Hill and left her laughing. Further up the street a man shouted at the sight of him and invited him in. He took off his Cossack hat, wiped his shoes, disappeared inside. His agent was worried about the time. 'The Doc hasn't had a cup of tea since dinner hour.' It was still raining. I asked Wesley to play 'The Sash' to cheer us all up and the agent told me that I'd rather have 'The Soldier's Song.'

Paisley continued his relentless rounds, but at five to eight he decided to leave, jumped into the jeep, then jumped out again to lock a garden gate. No, he told a policeman, he would not be going to Dunlow. 'Let the Prime Minister speak there.' And he drove off to the first of two open-air meetings twenty miles away.

In Wood Green the crowds gathered for a night's craic. They pour out of cars, tapping their toes to the Lambeg beat. Massive Union Jacks wave in the breeze. At the far end of the village a fife-and-drum band plays 'No Surrender' and Paisley, sash across his chest, smiles across his face, comes striding in. We're dancing with delight, we're people now, and the men talk of B Specials, Craig, and the alien master Chichester-Clark. 'Sure, he won't be able to do much, he's only one man, but he'll tell them what we're thinking, he won't let them away with things any more.'

Paisley gives a rousing speech and promises full use of

the parliamentary privilege. He quotes a number of houses without water. 'But nothing,' he says 'can stop the rising tide of Loyalist opinion.' He answers every question afterwards.

'Chichester-Clark says you're not British, Doctor Paisley.' Paisley snorts dismissively. 'Isn't that ridiculous?' and we laugh, and know they'll tell any amount of lies on him, they're that frightened. He steps down in amongst the crowd. His mother sits inside the jeep, waiting on her son to go to a local house for tea. He is very open and intimate and the men stand more proud and convinced after talking to him, and the women cluster around him, nodding their heads and giving him little white envelopes. He thanks them. He is confident and bulky in the dark and quotes the Bible and it is very reassuring. He sends you away with a joke and you aren't afraid any more. You can't be wrong if you're on the side of God and Ulster, with this big strong man in front of you. No one will sneer at you when the Reverend is around.

And that's Ian Paisley, Protestant preacher man, possible and improbable MP. For a wrathful God and an orderly Ulster where all the men are sinners and the wages of sin are death. In Christ Crucified is Salvation. Then he grins and you don't feel so bad about it.

OUR STREET

THE IRISH TIMES
MAY 1970

O nce everybody in our street used to vote for Eddie McAteer and sing 'Seán South' and hate the Corporation and enjoy the bands on the Twelfth, and Belfast was a place where you might get work, and if you were a Protestant you might get work, and if you were a Protestant you would somehow be better off, but you hadn't as much chance of getting to Heaven; and we wished for a United Ireland, although Dublin in the South was a foreign place, and if you became a teacher you were somebody; at least you were sure of always getting a job.

Last year our street split—fanatically—between Eddie McAteer, John Hume and Eamonn McCann, and the more progressive among us agreed that if Derry seceded to the South, Eddie would lead the charge across the bridge, waving his family allowance book; and who wanted to be a teacher when Du Pont paid thirty pounds a week, and Dublin didn't help us much in August and we hated Stormont, and we heard of the slums in Fountain Street and we welcomed the British troops, and we sang 'We Shall Overcome.'

There are spinsters in our street who broke their hearts and they stayed at home because they couldn't marry a Protestant. But several young people in our street have now made mixed marriages, although significantly they all married outside the parish and then moved out of town.

There used to be big nights in our street when a long-lost relative came home from America, and the women would sip sherry and the men would drink stout, and we would lean over the banisters and listen to them singing 'The Isle of Innisfree' as we thought of John Wayne and Maureen O'Hara, and afterwards they would go out into the street and bang pots and pans and sing 'Auld Lang Syne'. My aunt used to tell me how she shovelled coal into the boilers in the States, and I couldn't believe it, looking at her fur coat. I preferred the story of Captain Bounty who made his fortune in coconuts; and even though he kissed her toes, my aunt preferred to marry her Joe from Derry who worked on the railroad.

Some things, it seems, never change. In 1835 the Ordnance Survey of Derry recorded that, 'no calculation can be made of the large sums sent to residents of Derry from abroad ... no chance of place or habit interfere with the ties of consanguinity which bind the Irish emigrant to those whom he had apparently deserted.' But we don't have so many big nights any more. There are charter flights to America, only hours away, and we go and visit them.

Our street has a communal telephone and a communal car. The initial advantage for the telephone owner of not stirring from the fireside has rebounded somewhat, since he is continually running up and down the street saying 'Maggie has just phoned from England, and wants to talk to you,' or answering the door to a neighbour who wants to phone Jimmy in Scotland. The communal car belongs to the neighbour who takes you to the hospital when you've broken your leg, or takes your friend home on a very rainy night. The car owner is invariably described as being 'wild obliging.'

Our street has a communal shoulder, Mrs Barber, on whom one leans in times of stress, a communal source of miraculous relics, Mrs Doran; one for every illness, a communal genealogist, Ettie, who knows everybody and their ancestors and descendants, a communal handyman George, who can fix things and paint your house, a communal mother, mine, who gives out pieces of bread and jam, a communal seamstress, Tessie, who always has thread, and a communal source of cheap shirts, Annie, who works in the factory. We have a communal midwife, Nurse McBrearty, who gets babies direct from God, cutting out the middleman and transport expenses. Thus, I only cost my mother five pounds.

Mary-across-the-street has a lot of children and has to get up early, so she is our communal alarm clock, and Brigid-up-the-street keeps the keys and pays the debts of neighbours who go away on holiday. We even have a communal joke—on the day when pooled resources could not spell diarrhoea, Mamie sent a note to the teacher saying, 'wee John, big shite.'

Our street has a communal centre outside Ettie's door, where the women gather to chat after lunch hour on all but the worst days. They sit on chairs, on mats, or lean against the wall. If you approach Ettie's door from the foot of the street, your ancestry is established before you've passed the first house. Two more doors and we know your man's job and the number of your children. By the fifth door, your skeleton walks beside you, within earshot your health is questioned, and as you arrive we ask you 'What's new?'

The men in our street meet round the corner at night and out of sight in George the bookie's shed. We have never found out what really goes on there. But we are working on it.

Since it was first built, only three houses in our street have changed tenancy. We acquired snob status when permission to convert a house into a sweetshop was refused on the grounds that we were a residential area. Since the arrival of a new neighbour Gerald, a male nurse in a nerves clinic, we have discovered that we suffer now from acute depression as opposed to being simply fed up.

In our street there was no surprise when Patsy completed six months training as an apprentice plumber at the Government Training Centre, and then did six months on the dole before catching the boat to England. There is relief about the new houses, and cynicism about the absence of new jobs. There are great memories of last year and worries about this year. Our street doesn't really want to go back on the streets; but the men don't want to go back onto the street corner.

HER MAJESTY'S DERRY

THE IRISH TIMES
DECEMBER 1970

Because of unemployment and subsequent emigration there is a noticeable absence in Derry of bachelors in their early twenties. Consequently, those girls who have not yet 'got a man' hail the arrival of the forces enthusiastically and it is a pleasure to be wined and dined without regard to the 'Buroo Budget' or Social Welfare.

Derry is famed as a run-ashore port. The pubs are many and the girls are glad. Americans come first in the marriage stakes, but the arrival of the six-foot Grenadier Guards has somewhat evened things up. For the really discerning there are the RAF officers at Ballykelly, and the difficulties of distance, transport, and entry to their social club seem to be but minor deterrents.

The British sailor fared badly during the war years; he had nothing to offer but his pale maleness, which at that time was superabundant, while the Canadians had silk stockings and the Americans had dollars. But after the war, when the steep rise in illegitimate births was attributed mainly to the Americans, the British forces became rather more acceptable.

That the British naval presence has never aroused anti-British feelings in what is generally regarded as a Nationalist town is due to two factors. The naval base is situated across the river on the fringe of the Waterside and thus is outside the daily life of the city. When the sailors 'come ashore' they normally don civilian clothes. More importantly perhaps, the Navy has never been used to quell any rebellion or mix in the internal affairs of the town. The sailor comes, drinks, dances, and goes.

The British Army on the other hand is pursuing a shaky course. They arrived last August as saviours of the beleaguered Bogsiders. In their 'hearts and minds' campaign they undertook to provide recreational facilities for the youth of the city: a display of interest and attempt at integration which none of the services had ever shown before. But all this is continually offset on the Catholic side by the harsh semi-curfews they have imposed on Bogside residents every time the temperature has risen, and on the Protestant side by the fact they have replaced RUC control of the city.

MY MOTHER'S MONEY

∞∞∞∞∞∞∞∞∞∞∞∞∞∞∞∞∞∞∞∞∞∞∞∞

THE IRISH TIMES
MARCH 1971

T he way my mother sees it, 'they' have her beaten every time. She sat with her grocery book on Saturday night and worked out her weekly bill. The shopkeeper had marked the goods in 'English' prices, as she calls them; but the total, line by line, was marked in decimals.

My mother calculated, with pencil, glasses, currency converter and the blank edges of *The Belfast Telegraph* that she was being diddled to the tune of a halfpenny a line, but by the end of the page she was out tenpence, in pounds, shillings and pence, that is.

Then she added the total up in 'English' money. The three pounds eighteen was easy enough. No diddling there. And on the extra threepence, she lost only three-fifths of a penny. So my mother wants her total in 'English' money from now on, and she'll convert it herself.

Then there's the coalman. He charges her nineteen and ninepence per bag of coal. If she gives him a pound, he will give her a penny change. Thus, she loses a ha'pence per bag. He told her that wouldn't break her. No, she pointed out, but with five hundred customers, those extra halfpennies will make him richer to the tune of one pound tenpence per week.

'So what do you want me to do?' says he, 'Divide a bag of extra coal among five hundred customers?' My mother sat in the house on Saturday night and thought over the problem.

He can give the bag to an old age pensioner, she decided in the early hours of Sunday morning.

My mother is currently working on the difference between the banker's converter and the shopper's currency converter. Apparently the bankers get more value. She is using proper notepaper to work out that system. And she hums 'I'm the dame who broke the bank at Monte Carlo.'

DERRY'S SOLDIER DOLLS

THE IRISH TIMES
NOVEMBER 1971

'We're all terrorists now!' was a closing remark at an anti-internment meeting organized by the Socialist Resistance Group in Derry last August. Last week in Derry the middle classes entered the arena. At a public meeting of four hundred ratepayers in the city comprising business and professional people—architects, lawyers, dentists, doctors and ex-public officials—a resolution deploring violence from whatever quarter was defeated overwhelmingly .

Nor was any regret expressed at the tarring and feathering of Martha Doherty two days earlier. Violence as a way of life is accepted by all. The eminently respectable committee which raises funds for the internees now sells framed rubber bullets as souvenirs.

On Friday, the local Catholic paper, which has condemned violence in the past, along with the IRA, Communism and all things anti-establishment, carried not one single word of condemnation from any source of the punishment meted out to the girls who befriended soldiers. The front page carried the story and pictures, but discreetly left out the girls' names.

There were, however, statements from both wings of the IRA, denying responsibility for the incidents, but re-emphasizing warnings against fraternization. Regrets for the incidents are, by and large, confined to the method and not the principle of punishment. In a confused and confusing situation in this city, where no one group has the erstwhile overall authority of former Civil Rights days, the judgment is that a freelance women's revenge group translated more sanctions against the girls into 'excessive and unauthorized action.'

But that action has been judged in the context of three years of horrific and continuing violence against a people who have suffered political, economic, police and military oppression, and to whom the tarring and feathering of two girls came a short time after the death of a mother of five children. The close time sequence of the events—the killing of a woman by soldiers, and the punishment by other women of girl friends of the soldiers—is seen as wiping out any more comparisons.

In Derry they're saying that when Kathleen Thompson was shot, Army personnel said over the radio, 'I hope she's dead.' Later, they claim, the following Army message was broadcast: 'The score is civilians three, military nil, we are now playing into injury time. The Army marksman will be awarded five hundred Embassy coupons.'

The people to whom I have talked about this were incensed. I have no reason to doubt the truth of their statements, or the accuracy of their hearing. I myself heard some other sentiments broadcast by the Army following the death of William McGreanery some weeks ago.

The day after Kathleen Thompson's death, the IRA issued a final warning against fraternization. 'The time has come for action,' the warning said. Posters were put up in the Bogside condemning the soldiers as judge, jury and executioner of the people, and the people themselves then became judge, jury and executioner of girls who befriend such soldiers. And what Solomon will judge the moral, military and political morass into which Derry has subsequently plunged?

33

Derry has long been a garrison town. The American communications centre in the Waterside provides much-needed jobs and husbands in a city with 20 per cent male unemployment. When the British naval base where troops are now stationed was closed, the Nationalist Party led an outcry at the loss of ancillary civilian jobs.

When troops came to replace the Navy, they were welcomed with smiles and cups of tea as defenders of the minority; and the Catholic Church gave them their first base in the Bogside—on school grounds. The children have since been subjected to CS gas, rubber bullets and, their parents say, vicious verbal abuse.

Martha Doherty met her fiancé in those happy, post-riot days of 1969. No one objected then to his being a soldier. No one that I could find objected seriously when she was tarred and feathered last week. In the intervening days before the second girl was punished, the IRA could have—yet didn't—take action against unauthorized groups.

But the IRA is not alone responsible for the area. The Bogside, Brandywell, and Creggan are currently administered by three tenants' organizations, two women's action committees, five political groups, and autonomous street defence committees. They have no unified political or civilian voice, but they do have one clearly defined enemy, the British Army outside the Pale, and one clearly defined objective: survival.

'This is no time to talk of civil liberties,' a man who had watched the tarring and feathering told me. 'You get civil liberties in the political situation. This is no political situation. This is a war. If these girls who go out with soldiers never consciously give any information, every word they say is a piece in the military intelligence jigsaw.

'And even if they never said anything, they're giving comfort to an army which comes into this area nightly to fight with the people. Man, woman and child, no one is safe. People are dying, people are being interned; children who go to school learn that their classmate was killed the day before.

'We spent the last three years on the barricades night after night, protecting who against what? So these girls can sail safely through with soldier boy friends? Have you any idea what we've gone through, you who make moral judgments from the comfort of Dublin and London?

'That firm that sent wigs to the girls who were shaved, what have they sent to the children of Kathleen Thompson? Sweet damn all. Nor do they give a God's curse about the soldier's doll. They're looking for publicity. The outside world asks for normal standards. What human beings can live with death and destruction, day in, day out, and remain normal? The girls who comfort soldiers or the girls whose fathers and brothers have been taken away by soldiers?

'What does normal mean anyway? Jesus Christ Himself couldn't stick it. He asked for the bitter cup to be taken away, and he had only three days to suffer. We've gone through it now for three years. There's pressure weighing on us like the lid on a boiling pot.

'There are 35,000 people in this area, and not one of them feels safe. They could lift anybody. They could shoot anybody. And they have done so. And you want to worry about the judicial refinement regarding the trial of three girls who have been out having a good time!'

*   *   *

And what were those judicial refinements? Deirdre Duffy's mother wants to know, 'if any of their sons died for Ireland, those women who did this to my daughter?' Her son, John, died in the Bogside ten years ago at age sixteen, of self-inflicted accidental wounds while cleaning a revolver. His death is mourned by the Official IRA annually.

But last week her seventeen year-old daughter was shaved, tarred, covered in red lead, and tied to a lamp post. Deirdre's maternal grandfather served in two World Wars as a British soldier. Her paternal grandfather was a much respected police sergeant who served in the Bogside as a member of the Royal Irish Constabulary. Her paternal grandmother, a Protestant, became a Catholic. Her brother, Hugh, was a civil rights activist.

Deirdre's mother brought up five children on a widow's pension of nine pounds fifty a week, eking out the allowance by working as a charwoman day and night. By Derry standards the family is a credit to her: both sons working in a trade, a daughter married and actually housed, and another daughter educated through technical school working as a secretary.

And then Deirdre herself, the outgoing, friendliest member of the family who liked to dance? The soldiers offer the only place in Derry to dance nowadays and her dancing went on. But Derry standards last week dictated that she danced with the wrong tribe. She should have gone across the Border four miles away to the dance hall there, she said.

She had been repeatedly warned. Factory girls, with whom she had worked, had punched and beaten her. One of them was present at her trial last week. I know her well. I taught her at school. I watched her march for demands that she was told by public opinion were right. I watched her fight in 1969 when she was also told by public opinion that she was right. And I have seen her on the barricades defending the area against soldiers, told again that she was right.

But back in 1969, Deirdre and her friend were told it was right to befriend those same soldiers. To live in Derry now is to know only what is wrong—to know that street lights are out, that jobs are out, that amusement is out, that life itself can be wiped out if you are in the wrong place at the wrong time. In this tribal context public opinion states that it is wrong to step outside and claim the right to enjoyment with those whom your tribe has said is the enemy.

Tribe is a primitive word, war is a primitive situation and the civilized judgments from outside have no meaning here. Derry is no mean city and its people are not mean. By what means now can Derry be judged? 'You have to live here to know,' said Mary Duffy.

And several Derry girls after last week's incidents have chosen to live here no longer. Some left with their families, some alone.

One girl's father, a railway worker, stopped the train as it left Derry and asked his daughter to come home. She refused. She was going away to England, she said, leaving this bitter place to marry her soldier. She was eighteen years of age. Some of the girls going with soldiers, though not many, have remained behind. I asked one, a nineteen year-old, if she would continue to see her boy friend. 'Yes, I will,' she said, 'Even the IRA is saying now that they will not condemn girls who are in love with soldiers. I'm in love with mine.

'I met him in the beginning of 1970 when he was on foot patrol through the city. I brought him home and my parents liked him and the neighbours liked him, and nobody had a word to say against him then.

'It wasn't the British Army started the trouble in Derry. It was the police, and I hate the police. It was the Stormont Government, and they brought in the soldiers to clear up the mess left by the police. My boyfriend doesn't agree with the situation here but he can't understand why the Bogsiders have turned against him now. He's only doing his job and I know he's a good boy.

'I think the Army have been wrong some times. But so were we. The soldiers are tortured all the time with people shouting at them, throwing stones at them, and shooting at them, knowing quite well that the Army's not allowed to fire back. Sure the Army has the odd bad soldier in it, but there's bad people in Derry too.

'My boy's parents think that Ireland should be free and wish that he wasn't over here to do the dirty work of the Unionists. I don't think anybody remembers any more what started this all off in Derry. I don't know, and I don't know any more what we're looking for. All I know is I love my fellow and he's kind to me and he loves me and he even wishes we could settle in Ireland, at the Ballykelly camp or somewhere.

'Look at all those Derry girls who married soldiers before this and there's some of them now who've been living with their husbands in Derry for a long time. Nobody tells them they're wrong, because they met their boyfriends when Derry was peaceful. Well, I met my boyfriend when Derry was peaceful and I'm not giving him up now. I didn't start this, neither did he. But we're left in the middle and hated by everybody because they don't know who else to hate.'

Her mother said, 'I'm all mixed up. I'm on the side of the Bogside against anybody that attacks us, but I know Tom is a good fellow, I can't tell my daughter how to rule her own heart. I can see a case being made against the informers, but sure my wee girl is no informer and well they must know it.

'But I'm in fear now that they'll come for her, for who would dare to take her side? Everybody knows there was wrong done last week. Didn't the IRA themselves say the revenge group shouldn't have done it and didn't they say wee girls have a right to love?'

The family, she said, would not remain in the Creggan estate. The Commission had offered them a house out of the area and they moved to the other side of the river. She was in tears. 'I'll be leaving all my friends, but who has friends at times like this? Everybody is afraid to speak up in case their turn comes next.

'They say you can't have friends in a war. It's me that knows it this good day.'

COAT TALES

THE IRISH TIMES
DECEMBER 1971

A specialist in women's fashion once said of me, 'Whenever you see Nell at a press conference, you don't know whether to give her a handout or a penny.' She was referring to the fact that I am the worst-dressed journalist, if not female, in Dublin.

It was an amusing remark, passed in sympathy with the fact that I am pathological about clothes. I do not like to buy them. If they are offered to me by kind friends and they fit, I wear them gladly. Otherwise I make do with what I have. To allay the dismay of friends, I take them aside and tell them the story of my few coats over many years, with dresses not to match. Here, readers, is my story. I think it might make you cry.

When I was eight years old and my father worked in England—reader, are you crying yet?—my mother's rich American sister sent us a parcel of clothes that had been collected by her cinema-manager husband late at night in the cinema, after people left them behind.

The Irish always look after their relatives back home. Anyway, one day a parcel arrived in which there was an emerald green coat, fur-lined and with brown buttons. It was given to me. I was a sickly child, about to make my Confirmation. It being cold, the coat was over my former First Communion dress, and I was taken away to be slapped on the cheek by the bishop and made a soldier of Christ.

My coat was lined with medals: Sacred Heart, Virgin Mary, Saint Philomena (now demoted), Roy Rogers medallion, and hairy scapulas scratching my not yet nubile chest. After the boring ceremony, I went up the lane behind our street and began to play marbles.

It was the beginning of the season. I had bought some beautiful marbles in Woolworth's with my Confirmation money collection, which was not as bountiful as my first Communion collection. I kept the marbles in my white bag along with my rosary beads. I lost a few games, attributing it to my dog.

He recovered, so did I. We were a sacred trio, my dog, my coat and I. We stayed together, played together, prayed together. We loved each other truly.

One day my dog died. My mother put a Wagon Wheel chocolate biscuit in my pocket and sent me to see *The Wizard of Oz* in the cinema where my aunt was manageress.

I pined for a while, and they decided I was growing up. They decided to dress me up according to the advice of the fashion editor in *Women's Own*, to relieve my depression. Coming home from convent school one grammar-filled afternoon, I changed out of my uniform and sought my lucky coat. I was due to play handball on the gable at the foot of the street with my best friend Joe.

I went out to the tool shed where my coat was kept, and it was not there. 'Nell,' my mother told me in her wisdom, 'Today we go to Paddy Bannon's, and we get you a new coat.'

'Where's my lucky coat?' said I.

'I gave it to the ragman,' she told me.

'Where is the ragman?" I said.

'Going the rounds,' she replied.

I went to the foot of the street and told Joe. We went to look for the ragman. Up and down many streets we roamed, asking people if they had seen the ragman. We found him, finally. I asked for my coat. He refused. I said all my medals were on it, and looking him in his Catholic eye, I got my coat back.

Two weeks later, before a game of baseball, my persistent mother said she had given my coat to the binmen. She had bought me a new school blazer complete with proud coloured badge. I went looking for Joe. We got the binmen and their lorry, and my friend Joe climbed inside; after some time he emerged, Pal Joey with my lucky coat. I wore it all the way home. My mother said it had germs and could not henceforth be worn. I asked her to wash it. She did. Then one day, there was no coat. I do not know what happened to it. Nor did I miss it. It just fell off, I guess.

Then I acquired, in my lovelorn adolescence, a powder-blue overcoat trimmed with Afghan fur. That was ten years ago, remember, before Katmandu was heard of.

I went into the pub that night and everybody, but everybody, bought me a drink saying my coat was gorgeous, and I was carried home bleating like a lost Afghan lamb. The law student of my fancy subsequently married my best friend whose coat was paid for in cash at C&A. There just ain't no justice.

Life then became a suntanned glorious blank, because I went abroad to the hot places where one does not need a coat. I spent my days on Greek islands in a bikini and at night I wore two towels sewn together.

This went for on a long time, two years actually. I came home then, and went on the dole in Derry. Being a Catholic, I could always live at home, and gladly, since Derry people love their mothers to the point of idolatry. One night I was resisting another law student. Within a few more minutes I was in flames, since he had me backed up against an electric fire. Several hours later Derry was in flames, so my sister thought I had been a hero in her coat.

I saved up my dole money and bought what I considered to be the ultimate in coats—simple but devastatingly elegant navy-blue wool with a slit up the back and buttons on the sleeves. I looked girlish, slim, dark, and interesting, with just a hint of superiority. I flaunted that coat around town, reminding the bishop and bureaucracy that we, on the dole, could still retain our respectability. Even my mother was pleased.

That was two years ago. Today I still wear the coat, but the slit has become a tear. The armhole is verily an arm hole. There is one button to hold it together.

NUMBED AND RESTLESS

∞∞∞∞∞∞∞∞∞∞∞∞∞∞∞∞∞∞∞∞∞∞∞

THE IRISH TIMES
FEBRUARY 1972

How do you spend the day after thirteen people have been shot dead? For Free Derry it was numb exhaustion, an inability to sit down, a desire to keep constantly on the move, a grim seeking after details about the events of what we now call 'Bloody Sunday'.

Nobody worked. No children went to school. Some families do not know as yet where their sons, husbands, fathers fell. Nor have they retrieved their dead. They lie in Altnagelvin Hospital still.

Mickey, aged twenty, died when a bullet pierced his cheek and went out the back of his head. Five times on Sunday night, his family saw him singing and shouting on the television screen, but between newsreels his sister tried frantically to contact their scattered family in Wales, Rugby, Strabane, and Buncrana, County Donegal, to tell them of his death.

Throughout the last thirty-six hours the few phones in Bogside have been inundated with calls from relatives in far-off places asking to speak to their families up the street or round the corner. Neighbours congregate in each other's houses, often simply walking in with a pot of tea to help out in the crowd.

Rossville Street and the maze of courtyards off it where the boys were shot down was like Calvary and the stations of the Cross combined, a man said. Here he fell, there he called for help, here he was kicked, there he died. And there. And there. The blood-stained Civil Rights flag remains on the ground below the high flats, pinned down with a rosary of flowers. And placed on top of it in an open matchbox, the ghastly remnants of an eyelid complete with eyelashes, the remains of the man who died there.

There is a merciful threshold of tolerance beyond which limits the mind refuses to reach. Several times since 4.15 pm my mind has gone blank. Others confirm the experience. Did I really see a paratrooper shoot at a girl with a Red Cross uniform? Like everyone else I went back to look. On the wall of the courtyard where I sought shelter in a house there are two deep holes, reminders of the bullets that missed. Like Doubting Thomas, I put my fingers into them and checked the diagonal line between the holes, the girl's position in the middle of the square and the paratrooper's position at the far corner.

And then there were the things one had not known about. Six bullet holes in a single window pane of a second storey flat. Discarded shoes, coats, gloves. The abandoned houses on the perimeter where soldiers had taken up their firing positions. In retrospect you realize that you were not safe anywhere in that whole area.

We walked and talked in circles yesterday, and we smoked and went home for cups of tea and came out again. Sometimes it hits you, this awful sacrifice that was made, and then it goes away again because there is no comparable experience to which you can relate it. It is comforting almost to hear strangers describe and make intelligible on radio, television and in newspapers the overall picture. It is awesome to hear about what we went through, but it's not enough. We go back relentlessly to the details, the personal experience, and then ask what can be done to bring it home to the outside world. There's talk of bringing a funeral to Dublin, to march from the Garden of Remembrance to the Dáil.

Beyond the Bogside, the town, it seems, has closed down. I watched six boys throw desultory stones at a foot patrol in Waterloo Square. Immediately a Saracen came out of the barracks, followed by six soldiers on foot. But the boys had run home. The soldiers took up positions anyway, aiming their rifles at a solitary granny who came walking down the street.

Yes, sir, that was telling us. As if we didn't already know. And these soldiers weren't even paratroopers.

DISRUPTION DAY

∞∞∞∞∞∞∞∞∞∞∞∞∞∞∞∞∞∞∞∞∞∞∞∞

THE IRISH TIMES
FEBRUARY 1972

The eight hundred and eighty-eight acres of Free Derry remain free. Forty of the forty-two entrances to the Bogside, Creggan and Brandywell remain barricaded. Two are left open for the convenience of residents. For the thirty thousand people living within this area, the Queen's writ has not run since 9 August 1971. No soldier, no policemen, no Stormont law-enforcement officer, has walked these streets since that time, and when they breached one small rubble barricade in Rossville Street in the Bogside on Bloody Sunday they did so on the run behind armoured tanks with rifles blazing, while people's backs were turned.

To gain one hundred yards of territory, the British Army had to kill thirteen men, wound sixteen others, and pin a girl against a wall with a massive Saracen.

That the Army could re-enter under similar conditions, no one in Free Derry doubts. But it is significant that last Wednesday when a newly arrived Army regiment took a wrong turn that led them into the Bogside, a statement was issued by the Army pointing out that the soldiers were unfamiliar with the area and had mistakenly entered it.

The fact remains that Free Derry is withstanding the siege of the British Army, the RUC, the Stormont and Westminster governments and that the siege has gone on longer than the original siege of 1689 when the thirteen Apprentice Boys closed the gates of the walled city against the invading army.

Below those walls now, the people have entered into more than a mere military engagement. No rent or rates are paid. Gas and electricity bills are largely ignored. Empty houses and flats within Free Derry are allocated on a first come, first served basis, and the Derry Development Commission is powerless to intervene.

*   *   *

Street committees have been set up to meet weekly and discuss how best to run their own affairs and control their own lives. Each street provides its own vigilante patrol, its own street lighting service unit to replace lamps smashed by the Army, and its own first aid equipment. Elementary first aid classes are taught by qualified nurses.

The Brandywell has outshone everyone by providing night classes for the studiously inclined; lessons held in a small hut range from 'how to look after yourself' to 'how to embroider a tea cosy.' All military communications are carefully monitored on transistor radios and cars. People whom the British Army observe from vantage points outside the area are quickly warned by a verbal bush telegram.

A simple system of shouting from street to street ensures that boys in the front line are immediately warned that they have been identified or located. Barricades range from the sublime to the ridiculous. On the main street, cars and scaffolding and large blocks of stone have been firmly cemented into scooped-out trenches. The residents of one street in Creggan have procured an electronic pole light device, which is wired to a nearby lamp post. It seems to lift up and down at will, but is very nice. Little cone-shaped lamps on the road in front flash on and off, and in Creggan Heights a twenty-foot watchtower has been erected on scaffolding from which a powerful searchlight sweeps the fields beyond where the British Army sometimes patrols unapproved Border roads. The metal huts formerly used by workmen on building sites have been appropriated as shelters for the vigilantes and coal for the braziers is collected from houses nightly.

Street art has improved enormously since the bare slogans first daubed on walls in 1968. An amateur artist has done a series of huge wall painting around the Bogside apprising residents of anticipated British Army atrocities; one such line drawing in whitewash shows a soldier pointing his rifle at a baby in a pram. There's no need for a slogan. Politics and guerrilla warfare are the sole topics of conversation within the eight hundred and eighty-eight acres. Bogside children can expertly distinguish between the sounds of a nail bomb or gelignite, the sounds of a CS gas canister, a rubber bullet, or a rifle shot. Few people can remember the sound of a baton crunching a skull—that was four years ago.

There are good feelings and bad feelings. It is very good to wake up in the morning and wonder what you can do to hasten the destruction of Stormont today. Such 'power of the people' feelings are rare in a bureaucratized world. It is very bad to remember crawling on your stomach away from the paratroopers on Bloody Sunday. It was very good to march down the street and break the law and sing songs. It was very bad to see a wounded man outside the window and not dare go out to help him.

*   *   *

It was very good perhaps to see people from the South come north to demonstrate. It was very bad to see an ex-Cabinet Minister for Fianna Fáil agree in Newry that internment should be abolished in Ulster when he himself signed a permit order in the South where the Offences against the State Act still exists. It was very good, perhaps, to see three members of the Irish Labour Party defiantly break the Ulster law in Newry and strange to realize that not one of them had broken a southern law, which they also bitterly oppose—the Prohibition of Forcible Entry and Occupation Act.

And in Derry, the mood is very clear.

MARTIN McGUINNESS:
PROFILE OF A PROVO

∞ ∞

THE IRISH TIMES
APRIL 1972

'**Y**ou know how much life has changed when you're having a Republican tea—a bottle of orange and a bap—in the back of a car, just a few minutes from your own home.'

At twenty-one, Martin McGuinness, O.C. of the Derry Provisional IRA, may have changed his lifestyle. But he is acutely embarrassed at popular press descriptions of him as 'the boy who rules Free Derry.' He was catapulted into the limelight at a press conference in Creggan estate last week, and since then the English papers have had a heyday writing about his 'good looks, youth and shy charm.'

An American TV man spent a wistful hour planning the scenario for a colour-film spectacular about him. 'Jeez,' he said, 'that boy would be hot on the coast. Can you see him, six feet tall in a dinner jacket, raising funds?'

His wish will, presumably, not be granted. The English journalist who romanticized Mr McGuinness was ordered out of town. He left immediately.

'I don't feel like a big shot, travelling around the area in a stolen Ford Avenger,' said Martin. 'I have to do what the people want. They don't treat me like I was something different. In fact one wee woman couldn't understand why I couldn't go down to the police barracks to bail out her son who'd been arrested. I had to take her up to headquarters and arrange for someone else to do it.'

He joined the IRA after the Battle of the Bogside in 1969. Initially he was with the Official wing. 'There wasn't a Provo unit in Derry then. The Officials approached me and for three months we attended policy and training lectures in a house in the Bogside.

'But they wouldn't give us any action. All this time, there was fighting in the streets and things were getting worse in Belfast. You could see the soldiers just settling into Derry, not being too worried about the stone-throwing. Occasionally the Officials gave out Molotov cocktails which wouldn't even go off, and I knew that after fifty years we were more of an occupied country than we ever were before.

'It seemed to me that behind all the politics and marching it was plain as daylight that there was an Army in our town, in our country, and that they weren't there to give out flowers. Armies should be fought by armies. So one night I piled into a black Austin, me and five mates, and we went to see a Provo across the Border. We told him our position and there were several meetings after that. Then we joined. Nothing really happened until Seamus Cusack was killed and internment came soon after. Then the Provos in Derry were ordered into full-time military action. I gave up my job working in the butcher's shop.'

His mother was panic-stricken, he said, when she found out that he was in the IRA. 'A few months after I'd joined she found a belt and beret in my bedroom and there was a big row. She and my father told me to get out of it, and for the sake of peace I said I would, and they calmed down. But now they have to accept it. They've seen the British Army in action and they know I'd no choice.'

His mother, though, had started smoking again, which she hadn't done in years. 'I know her health has failed and she's always worrying about me. If I'm not around to tell her myself I send her word that I'm all right. I don't discuss my business with her and she doesn't ask.'

Martin's mother was angry at the press reports of him. 'You'd think he was running around the area with a gun, telling people what they could and could not do. The only time I saw guns in this house was when the British Army raided it.' She worries about him even more since Joseph McCann was shot in Belfast.

'Since Martin's picture appeared in the papers every soldier in Derry knows what he looks like.' And when it's all over—should it ever end—she worries about his job. 'His trade's been interrupted. His father is a welder, his brothers bricklayers and carpenters, but what will become of Martin? That's why they'll have to get an amnesty so's he can get back to work and not be always on the run.'

Martin himself doesn't worry too much about what will come after. His aims are devastatingly simple.

'I want a United Ireland where everyone has a good job and enough to live on.' He had read a little, he said, since becoming a Republican, and supported Socialist views, 'but the Officials are all views and no support. I wish we were getting more press coverage in Derry for our political beliefs but we don't have the talkers in our ranks. Still, the people support us and that's good enough.'

He wondered sometimes, he said, if Socialism would ever work out. 'I have a lot of respect for Bernadette Devlin but I think maybe people are too greedy. I'd be willing to sweep the roads in my world and it wouldn't seem like a bad job if they got the same wages as everybody else, but do you not think now that people are just too greedy? Somebody always wants to make a million. Anyway, before you can try, you have to get this country united.

'We'd make sure that Protestants are fairly treated. Don't accept that we are sectarian. But you have to face facts that it's the Catholics who've been discriminated against. The Officials go on about us all the time but it was them that blew up the Protestant mayor's house in Derry and shot Barnhill and John Taylor. Mind you, I've nothing against the rank and file Officials. They're soldiers just like me, with a job to do. That job, as far as I am concerned, is to fight the British Army.'

The Provisionals took care, he said, not to harm innocent civilians. 'But sometimes mistakes are made. There was an explosion in Derry some time ago, and I read afterwards that a man had been trapped in the basement. He lost a part of his leg. Then you read that he's a cyclist and you feel sad.

'The worst I ever felt was Bloody Sunday. I wandered about stunned, with people crying and looking for their relatives, and I thought of all that guff about honour between soldiers. The British Army knew right well we wouldn't fight them with all those thousands of people there, so they came in and murdered the innocent.

'I used to worry about being killed before that day, but now I don't think about death at all.'

If there's a riot on, he sometimes goes and throws stones. 'It relieves the pressure and it's a way of being with my mates, the ones who have not joined the movement, and I feel just ordinary again.

'I suppose,' he added, 'you think us Provos have no feelings at all just because we have no time to talk about it.'

Last week he talked publicly for the first time. His speech, to a wildly cheering crowd in the Brandywell, was very short and to the point. 'If Gerry Fitt and John Hume think they're going to sell the people out,' he said, 'they've got another thing coming. It's just not on.'

He looked very young as he spoke. He was probably not what Austin Currie had in mind last autumn when he warned the people that the possible imprisonment of MPs would create a need for 'second-tier leadership.' But the influential, middle-aged, middle of the road Derry Central Citizens Council took sufficient cognizance of his leadership to go and have a talk with him about his ideas. Afterwards they rejected Provisional proposals for elections in the city. Martin didn't mind too much.

'I know they're wrong,' he said. 'I know it and I feel it when I go round the barricades and see the boys they called hooligans, and the men they called wasters, and the fellows that used only to drink, doing things they really believe in now. Protecting the area and freeing Ireland and freeing themselves.'

VILLAGE IN THE MOUNTAINS

∞ ∞

THE IRISH TIMES
JUNE 1972

Sitting on a manure cart drawn by two magnificent muscle-bound white cows, their foreheads regally covered in sheepskin, I arrived in Ainhoa in the Pyrenees at high noon. We progressed at a stately pace, albeit creaking, up into the village and tethered at the Franco-Espagnole Bazar, the last stop before the frontier. My chauffeur swept off his black Basque beret, swept me onto my manure-spattered feet, and took me inside for a tot of rum in black coffee. A person needs sustenance in these here mountains, where there are no buses, taxis or trains. He drove me back to my hotel—a mere matter of yards—for the lack of oxygen had rendered me unsteady. I was given a room looking out on flower-spangled fields, with peaky ridges beyond the wooded green valley.

Ainhoa is a peaceful street of broad, wood-beamed, whitewashed houses with overhanging, sloped, red-tiled roofs. The ground floor quarters provide spacious barns for the cart and cows and pigs. Access to the upper storey is gained by a sealed-off narrow stairway. In front of the house you may take your ease on stone blocks or wooden benches, gathered round a crudely hewn low table. Ivy and climbing flowers are trained on the dazzling facades.

Above the lintel of the front of the door is inscribed the date of construction, and the family history: 'Martin Varian —Catherine Dirube, joined together 1854. This house, called Gorritia, was bought by Maria de Gorriti, mother of Jean Dohageray, with money sent by him from the Indies. This house may not be sold or rented. Built in 1662.' In one century alone, the Basques exported 90,000 of their children to the Indies and Latin America.

In the little graveyard of the church, the family tombstones trace the lineage back to the sixteenth century. At the church door a notice politely bids men who wish to assist at devotions to mount to the three galleries, women to congregate in the well around the altar.

The southern wall of the cemetery drops onto a scooped-out square below and forms the high gable wall of the pelote alley. On Sunday afternoon, and sometimes in the evening after work, the men gather in teams to play pelote, a form of handball, using a long wooden claw attached by a leather glove to the wrist. They play in white shirts and trousers with coloured waistbands to denote their teams and shout 'Ho!' when they are about to begin, which is useful for people like me who cannot keep track of the whizzing ball.

At sunset and indeed often earlier, they fade back into their homes to watch television, which I can see throwing a silver glare through the rust-red shutters, on to the village dogs and me.

Nothing daunted, the night of my arrival I hit the Franco-Espagnol Bazar, the toughest and, truth to tell, the only joint in town. There were six men, three calendars, seven tables and twenty-two chairs. The patron, a sprightly martinet, haltingly courteous, went to great pains to amuse me. I was supplied with rum and coffee and back copies of *Le Monde*, an excellent newspaper with many in-depth articles on the Indo-China struggle. His wife appeared silent and smiling from the back-kitchen, loaded with the magazines *Elle* and *Paris-Match* and a delightfully scandalous news-sheet called *France-Dimanche*. 'Mademoiselle likes to read,' the patron told the farmers. Actually mademoiselle was dying to join in their game of stud-poker, which they played using rounded pebbles as bets. I kid you not, I have seen mountain men gamble for stones and hesitate before raising the ante.

The bar closed at ten o'clock, and from my room I watched the stars, cold and many and clean. In the distance I could see the red warning glow of a television transmitter, the brightest light in the Pyrenees. I have decided, henceforth, to call myself Heidi.

The village zaps into life at sunrise, what with cocks crowing, cows lowing, sheep bleating under one's window. In the back gardens of the houses, the women tend vegetables, feed fowl, and raise rabbits. In the front street the men pass by with flocks and herds, and carts loaded with mown greenery, which may not be grass—probably hay, though I always thought that was yellow. They do not use tractors, which are too expensive for their small holdings and cannot negotiate the hill-slopes.

I spent my days on a bench outside the Bureau de Poste watching the world go by and ogling tourists in flash cars, lorries carrying stone from the quarry and BP-Zoom tankers bringing natural gas from the deposits in the foothills. The postmaster, broadly built and limping, with an iron-grey crew cut, joins me sometimes for a laconic conversation. He has given up smoking and relies on chewing gum. He finds it difficult to revert from the Basque dialect full of k's and z's and x's to the formal French with which he shyly interrogates me.

The children come up from school at four o'clock and set up a post office on the street, using toy telephones and old letters. Their mothers wash sheets at the village trough off the main road, which is *plus practique* than passing them through the washing machine. They do their sewing under a rectangle of elm trees, which have been lopped off at the top, the branches pulled down onto the crossbars to form a sunshade. Bread and chocolate is distributed for afternoon *goûter*.

The days pass gently so, until the weekend, when the youths come home from their jobs in the towns below. On a Friday night the young boys and girls dressed in white, the girls garlanded with flowers, assisted at the exposition of the Blessed Sacrament. They scattered rose petals in the aisle of the church, and played brass instruments with more enthusiasm than finesse. Afterwards the trumpets blared behind the tombstones in the dark, and we waited on the street until they had gathered themselves together for a musical march to the Mairie. The ceremony was toasted with Pernods all round, and I was invited to watch television until eleven-thirty. I saw an old film starring Gerard Philippe, the French Clark Gable.

We sat around the family dining table on straight-backed plain wooden chairs, gazing steadfastly at the TV set high up on a shelf on the wall. We did not speak.

*   *   *

On Saturday, a van arrived with fresh meat and sausage and wrapped cheese and vegetables to supplement the necessities sold at the two small general stores. At four o'clock in the afternoon, Laurent Munduteguy, motor-mechanic, married Jeannine Nogue, *femme de chambre*, at a civil ceremony in the Mairie. The thirty guests crowded into the room opening off onto the street, some spilling outside, but the windows were discreetly closed, affording privacy to the couple in front of the mayor's desk. At four-twenty they crossed the street and entered the church, the mothers weeping disconsolately, the fathers straight and bursting in their tight blue-serge suits.

Laurent was tall, narrow-waisted and slim-hipped,

with slender hands and a dark sleek cap of hair. He wore a cutaway suit with flared trousers, and a very white shirt. He seemed particularly proud of his grey gloves, with which he occasionally slapped his thigh. After the church ceremony, traffic was held up while he and Jeannine stood on a bench in the street, surrounded by relatives, and posed for pictures. They drove away then to the reception in a hotel by the river.

On Saturday night, the nine young bachelors of the village gathered in the café and sang Basque songs and religious chants lustily and harmoniously. I did not get to watch TV, as the sullen citified daughter returned in tears to get over a *crise d'amour*. The whole village was in bed by eleven, exhausted by this busy day.

Sunday was as Sunday is: Mass and newspapers and rain. I walked two miles to the Spanish border, where police and soldiers scrutinized my Irish passport and checked through a filing cabinet of indexed alphabetical reports and photographs. How long did I wish to stay, where would I sleep, how much money did I carry? I played the jukebox in a café and returned to France.

To break the routine, I decided not to dine off the usual thick soup, chicken, cheese and fruit. I went to a luxurious hotel at the end of the village street, where pale Parisians had come to breathe the mountain air and watch colour TV. I was a little late—nine o'clock—but they were gracious.

What a meal! A bowl of paté accompanied by crudités, dressed cucumber, tomato slices, grated carrots, beetroot cubes, ham and mussels served with rice. A fat trout cooked whole in butter followed. Then a silvery dish of mutton, with a small roast potatoes and spinach. The cheese board required its own table. Finally, a slice of cherry pie, with a side dish of cherries shining on a bed of green leaves. With a half-bottle of Bordeaux bottled in the hotel's own cellar, the bill came to one pound eighty, *service compris*. When I think of chop and chips in Dublin for twelve bob!

On Monday I studied the chickens and rabbits in the garden below my window and scratched my flea bites. Chickens are stupid and rabbits are passive, I decided after deep thought. On Monday night the border patrol arrested two Spaniards who were trying to smuggle 27,000 cigars in a lorry which crashed on the last French bend. The tinkling bells of frightened sheep gave them away. Ainhoa was getting too hot for comfort, so I took my suitcase in hand and started walking towards the Camargue, over near Marseilles where I believe there are cowboys to be seen.

IN THE EYES OF THE LAW

∞∞∞∞∞∞∞∞∞∞∞∞∞∞∞∞∞∞∞∞∞∞∞

NELL McCAFFERTY

I t is often said of courts that all human life is there. In the decade 1970-1980 that I spent in and around the court rooms of the Republic of Ireland as a journalist with *The Irish Times*, I saw an astonishing parade come to answer the rule of law. Babies were held in arms in the Children's Court as the Justice decided where they should go. Cabinet ministers appeared in the dock; eight year-olds who played football in the streets were brought in by guards and convicted; businessmen who assaulted each other in discotheques brought charges and countercharges. A mother of thirteen children who stole trousers for her unemployed husband received a suspended sentence.

Religion, sex and politics had a high profile. Members of the Hare Krishna movement were summonsed for walking in the streets; the Maoists were convicted of posturing and sent to jail for contempt, homosexuals were convicted; the State loitered in prosecuting a man charged with buggery, and he was released to molest two children before final conviction.

Entire families, decimated and estranged, appeared in the dock, and neighbours besides. Husbands who beat up their wives and avoided paying maintenance were occasionally assaulted by their wives. Parents summonsed their children; in-laws became outlaws after conviction.

Neighbours accused each other, friends assaulted each

other, some appeared surprised and confused after a night on the tiles. Winos and beggars were hauled in. Demented women, vague men and wandering children regularly trooped through.

There was real crime too—burglary, theft, forgery, stealing cars, all too often committed by men who began their careers in children's reformatories and were processed through St Patrick's, Mountjoy, Dundrum Mental Hospital and back to Mountjoy again, with occasional breaks in the fresh air and no hope of a life outside institutional walls.

The travelling people are regularly fined in pounds, shillings and pence, and then either released back to the bridges where they had begged, or sent to jail.

People are found innocent of charges originally brought against them, and then convicted of having resisted the guards in the course of arrest; or obstructing them, or assaulting them. A prison sentence is often imposed.

While waiting for the law to take its course in the midst of this bedlam, people apply for bail and freedom. The relatives who come to buy them out are refused because the father is not earning enough, the mother is earning nothing, the Credit Union book is rejected. Banks are thicker than blood.

The law is subject to the season of the year—around Christmas, the Justice promises jail for shoplifters—and it often depends on the personality of the Justice. One likes to jail drug addicts, another likes to put them under probation.

In the ten years that I spent in and around the courts, I learned that there is a clear distinction between law and justice. The parent who steals for food for the children is praised in parable and convicted in the court; the alcoholic who needs treatment is punished; the beggar who needs money is jailed. The person who goes to jail again and again and is not rehabilitated is sent back to the jail again and again and again.

Because these people have suffered more than enough by appearing in court in the first place, I never used their real names and addresses. I have named the Justices who decided their fate. Hopefully, this will have put them in the dock for a change. A change in the District Courts of this country is urgently needed.

In the Eyes of the Law (Dublin 1981)

PERSISTENT MAOIST
TAKEN TO CELLS

∞ ∞

THE IRISH TIMES
MAY 1973

'**S**tand up in Court,' the sergeant called as District Justice Ó hUadhaigh entered Dublin District Court Number Six. The District Justice was about to seat himself when the sergeant called out again, 'Stand up in Court, you.' The man at the back, who had just been released after serving seven days for contempt, remained seated. Then he raised himself a little, and the District Justice lowered himself a little. 'Stand up,' the sergeant called again and the man continued raising himself off his bench, as the District Justice proportionately lowered himself onto his chair. Bottoms poised in mid-air as the stage tensed. Finally, the man got up and the District Justice got down. Law and order was restored.

The man came forward then to answer charges. A member of the Communist Party of Ireland, Marxist Leninist, he was charged with selling literature without a street trader's licence, with assaulting the gardaí, resisting arrest, and obstructing the police in the due execution of their duty. The man had twice been sentenced for contempt of court, because he persisted in asking the gardaí why they had charged him with breaking a law when none of the public objected to his selling literature and indeed bought it off him, the man alleged.

'There's no need to repeat the evidence,' the garda began. 'Why not? I haven't cross-questioned yet,' the man replied. His Maoist badge was prominent on his lapel. 'Before you begin,' District Justice Ó hUadhaigh warned him, 'I can tell you here and now that the only questions allowed are those relevant to the issue.'

'That's what's been going on since I came before this court,' the man said. 'I have to put up with this sort of thing every time I'm brought here.' 'Do you intend to address the court now on the evidence, or continue questioning?' asked the District Justice. 'If you want to ask questions, cease the preliminaries and get on with it, please.'

'The conduct of this trial is in flagrant breach of your own laws. My arguments expose the nature of this court,' the defendant said.

'If you continue like this, I'll have to take a certain course,' the District Justice said.

'I'm going to question this lackey here,' the man said, pointing to the garda.

'Kindly stop that. If you proceed in this manner I'll have you removed to the cells, and continue the case in your absence,' the District Justice said.

'Fine,' said the man. 'That exposes the nature of this court even further.' The District Justice ordered the gardaí to remove him. A garda took the man by the shoulder, he called out 'Down with fascism!' and pulled away. Another garda caught him, and again he called 'Down with fascism!' and his arms were outstretched now, his feet spread-eagled. Two more gardaí grabbed him and he was taken down the steps to the cells below. There was much noise, and sounds came thumping off the wooden stairway, and then up from the cells came a cry 'Get off him, get off him, leave him alone!' Struggling thumping sounds, and the cry 'Down with fascism.'

The court waited in silence, and the cries and noises

came echoing up: 'Leave him alone, leave him alone, down with fascism, leave him alone, leave him alone!' The noises ceased. The court resumed its deliberations. A police inspector told how he had tried to reason with the defendant on the occasion of his arrest in Thomas Street, only to be told that he was 'arrogant'. The man refused to give his name and address and the sergeant had put his hand on his shoulder.

'You will not arrest me,' the man said as he put his hands on his head and called on passersby to help him 'resist the fascists'. There was a struggle and he and his companion were put into the patrol car.

The inspector produced the literature that was being unlawfully sold, and the solicitor asked with a smile if these books were copies of *The Thoughts of Chairman Mao*. The inspector agreed with a smile that they were, and the other gardaí involved in the case also smiled. At this point the court sergeant went to the back of the court and asked a member of the public to remove his feet from the bench in front of him.

All was present and correct and the District Justice proceeded to enunciate his thoughts. 'Well, we'll have to have that man brought up again, in fairness to him. I think, court sergeant, if you're of the opinion that he will continue to behave in the manner just exhibited, you may come back and tell me. I don't want the performance of ten minutes ago. If you're of the opinion that there will be difficulty getting him up the stairs, you can tell me.'

The sergeant disappeared down below and the cry came up 'Down with fascism!' and the sergeant came back up to report that 'this man will probably take whatever course he wants to'.

The District Justice observed that the defendant had by his own actions waived his right to a normal trial, and he convicted him. The garda said that the defendant had no

67

actual previous convictions. He had been charged once with an offence under the Public Meetings Act, had been committed for seven days for contempt and the case had not proceeded to conviction. The only other thing he knew was that the defendant had given his occupation as ' … rat catcher, though I find that rather hard to believe, Justice.' 'I know what he means,' the District Justice remarked.

District Justice Ó hUadhaigh said that anyone was entitled to expound political views, provided they were expounded within the laws of the State. But in his opinion this defendant had transgressed the law in order to be arrested and appear in court, thereby getting himself cheap publicity by the manner in which he behaved in court. Well, now he couldn't be allowed to do this at the expense of the citizens, and the gardaí had presented their evidence fairly, and he had no reason to disbelieve them. 'Unfortunately for the defendant, or maybe fortunately for him, this is a serious offence, meriting severe punishment,' and violence against the gardaí was endemic—obstructing, resisting, and assaulting them for reasons which the District Justice found mostly 'to be pure figments of the imagination.'

The District Justice could not tolerate attacks on 'the unarmed forces of the State,' and he sentenced the man to six months' imprisonment, and indeed if the man had had previous convictions, the District Justice said, he would have given him twelve months. The man's companion had been fined twelve pounds by District Justice Coglan two weeks ago for the same offences, District Justice Ó hUadhaigh was out of the city that day.

The next case involved a member of the same political party who the garda testified had been 'distributing pamphlets outside the GPO, carrying a red book and obstructing the path of passers-by'. The man first appeared on this charge six weeks ago; he had then pleaded 'not guilty to crime against the Irish people' and opposed the right of the a court to try him, and was subsequently given seven days for contempt by District Justice Ó hUadhaigh.

The man refused to move on when asked, the garda said, and had refused to give his name and address. The garda then arrested him. When the garda placed his hand on his shoulder, the man 'turned round, hit me on the body, caught hold of me, and when I held him on the ground had violently resisted me, and tried to incite a hostile crowd to resist the fascists and the imperialist government.'

The man asked the garda why he and his companion had been singled out from among the many groups of people selling or distributing literature outside the GPO that Saturday, and the garda replied, 'Most of them gave their names and addresses or had licences.' 'Why wasn't I arrested the following week when I was there again?' the man asked, and the garda said, 'I didn't see you.'

'I put it to you,' said the man, 'that this was part of a three-pronged government plan to attack us on three different occasions, at Westland Row, at the GPO and in Thomas Street, in order to wipe out, intimidate us, and prevent the sale of revolutionary literature.'

'I couldn't say that!' said the garda.

'You mean you can't,' replied the man,

'This is an ordinary garda,' said the District Justice.

'He's a fascist,' said the man,

'That is contempt,' said the District Justice.

'This is intimidation,' said the man.

The garda admitted that the crowd was hostile to the police and had said things like 'traitors' and 'bastards.'

'Do you claim to protect the people's rights therefore?' asked the man. The District Justice said the garda didn't claim this, but was only enforcing the law and he didn't have to answer the question. 'You mean he's no mind of his own?' asked the man. There followed an exchange between the District Justice and the man, with the

District Justice saying he wasn't going to bandy words, and that 'communist, fascist, nazi or democratic attack is not the issue here.

'It's the fascists who attack,' said the man. 'We are communists.'

When another garda was questioned by the man about the attitude of the crowd that had gathered round, the District Justice said that it was already proved that the crowd was hostile to the police, and the man said, 'So that proves we stand for the rights of the people.'

The defendant then addressed the District Justice, basing his right to sell or distribute literature on his political right to alert the people to imperialism and economic discrimination of the working class North and South. The District Justice stopped him eventually, pointing out that it was normal practice to allow such speeches in court only to people who were under sentence of death—and then only after sentence and conviction had been pronounced.

There were no previous convictions against the man, the garda said, but the District Justice remarked that the man had been before him on a previous occasion. The whole thing was serious, the District Justice thought, the 'unlawful circulation of propaganda by way of street-trading,' and the attack on and resistance and obstruction of the police, and he sentenced the man to six months in prison.

'Death to British Imperialism,' called the man as they led him below. 'Long live the Communist Party of Ireland, Marxist Leninist.'

BELLS AND SMELLS

THE IRISH TIMES
JUNE 1973

'They were walking down Grafton Street playing music and making a lot of noise. I had cautioned them on previous occasions not to play music to the annoyance of the inhabitants of the street. There have been serious complaints from the inhabitants, and they were making considerable noise. They were using cymbals and drums and bells. They were walking in single file but people had to walk in the roadway to avoid them.'

The detective concluded his evidence before District Justice Breathnach in Dublin District Court Six. The five accused people stood before the District Justice, gentle and smiling. They were all dressed in the now familiar pink, yellow and orange robes of the Hare Krishna religious sect. Their heads were entirely shaved, except for a short thin strand of pigtail growing from the backs of their skulls. Each had a pink cotton purse hanging from his wrist, in which were the beads they constantly fingered as they prayed. One boy disengaged himself from the proceedings and meditated happily, his lips fervently moving.

His companion, the only one to wear a cloth over his head, had a cylindrical drum suspended from his neck, to which was attached the musical bells beloved of orientals. The bells tinkled musically as he shifted his feet. 'Will you keep that thing quiet please?' snapped the District Justice. 'Take it off! Take it off!' commanded the court sergeant.

A brown-eyed youth studied the charges of the sheet in his hand. They had been collectively accused of 'using noisy instruments, to whit cymbals and drums for the purpose of distributing literature relating to a religious sect for the purpose of gathering people together.'

They were also accused of 'committing an offence, to whit marching in single file, playing instruments, and obstructing traffic.'

They were finally accused of 'insulting behaviour, whereby a breach of the peace may be occasioned.'

'We weren't obstructing traffic,' the brown-eyed youth said.

'Did they want to question the guard's evidence?' the District Justice asked. There was silence, and the District Justice asked the detective if they understood what he was saying.

'Do they speak English?' the District Justice asked uneasily.

'Oh yes, one comes from Wales, one from Trinidad, and the other three from Ireland,' said the detective. They said they didn't want to question the detective, but would like to defend themselves, without taking the oath.

'I'll just give my evidence from here, is that alright?' asked the boy.

That was alright.

'Well, as far as the charges go,' the first said, 'to draw people together and distribute literature. Now, nobody distributed literature. And we didn't get in anybody's way. We have been charged before, and the Justice told us last time that we should march in single file and not obstruct the highway, and that's what we did.'

'That's what the sergeant says, you obstructed traffic,' said the District Justice. 'Oh no, we didn't, we marched in single file along the gutter,' said the boy. 'We were simply walking along the side of the footpath, in single file, not getting in anybody's way, as far as I could see. There were not too many people around at the time. Nobody had to walk in the road.'

The others reiterated his evidence, and the boy from Wales said he had done this all over the world and no one had ever told him before that he was not allowed to do this.

The District Justice said he was satisfied they were guilty as charged. 'Why are you dressed up in those ridiculous garments?' the District Justice then burst out. 'We are monks,' the brown-eyed boy explained. 'I could sentence you for contempt, wearing a scarf like that in court,' the District Justice said.

'I understand they're a religious sect,' the detective explained, 'though of course I've no objection to them as such, it's just that they were playing instruments and collecting.' That was the first we'd heard of collecting.

'I can warn you that you are lucky not to have been assaulted by a crowd. Any decent Irishman would object to this carry-on,' District Justice Breathnach told these members of a religious sect that differs from the religion of the vast majority of Irishmen.

Does that mean that those of us who do not object are not decent? Or will a sympathetic view now be taken by the courts of those Catholic Irishmen who take it upon themselves to tear the Hare Krishna members limb from limb?

'They were warned on previous occasions to desist from this behaviour,' the detective said, restraining his sense of outrage.

'I've no jurisdiction to order a forfeiture of those things, bells and leaflets. If I had, I'd be fairly radical and confiscate those nonsensical things,' said the District Justice.

'Why do you say nonsensical?' asked the brown-eyed boy.

'Because you're disturbing the peace of this city, and

I'm sure my colleagues will agree with my only regret that I can't have you locked up,' said the District Justice.

'May I say something about our movement?" asked the boy.

'I don't want to hear anything about your movement, whether you keep stationary or not,' said the District Justice cleverly.

He then fined them a total of seven pounds each on all the charges. 'I can tell you,' finished the District Justice, 'that the only reason I'm not imposing heavier fines is that I don't have the jurisdiction … though I suppose I could increase the fine for obstructing the traffic and playing those instruments.'

Christian charity prevailed, however, and he let them go. The monks stood out in the courtyard afterwards, and some of the gardaí asked them for their leaflets. One guard asked them to play him a tune, remarking to me that 'they had drink and sex and everything in the houses where they lived.'

Another guard then asked them why they wore those ridiculous clothes that made them stand out. The boy pointed out that the guard's uniform was equally conspicuous and the guard said that he was paid to wear it. The boy pointed out that nuns and priests wore distinctive habits also, and the guard said they led good lives.

'I mean, look at that boy over there praying against a wall,' said the guard, pointing to the monk who was meditating.

'What's wrong with praying?' asked the boy.

'You should pray in church,' said the guard, 'and anyway the priests aren't prating all day.'

Earlier, District Justice Breathnach had fined a travelling woman who appeared in court with her baby swaddled in a blanket, charged with begging. The woman's husband was in jail. 'This is the tourist season,' said the District Justice, 'and it makes a bad impression on them to go back to their own countries with memories of having been accosted on the streets. They'll think we're a nation of beggars.'

That must be it. First, the Maoists; then the travelling people, now the monks of Hare Krishna—bring them into court and off the streets—keep Ireland Catholic and clean for the tourists. They'll be puttin' a curfew on Benburb Street next. I wonder what will happen to the Dublin shops that sell coloured cotton robes and musical bells?

As I crossed the bridge after the court session, I passed a shabbily dressed blind man playing a flute. Trying to be decent and in the majority, I restrained myself from throwing him over the bridge and into the Liffey. Luckily there were no tourists about.

SEX OFFENDER

∞ ∞

THE IRISH TIMES
JANUARY 1974

He had seen the defendant in the laneway with three juveniles, the guard told District Justice Good in Dublin District Court Number Four. He had no idea what they were doing at this time, and so did not stop the man when he first came out of the laneway and passed on up the square. The guard questioned the juveniles, who explained to him that the man had paid them some money and interfered with them.

The guard stopped the man when he returned to his car, and the man admitted that the information was correct and had made a statement later in the station. 'You say he interfered with them?' questioned the Justice. 'He had paid them to masturbate him,' explained the guard. He then read out the man's statement.

The guard said the three youths were itinerants aged ten to fourteen, and he had been unable to contact their parents, who were very hard to locate. He had seen the youths every night around the town 'begging and so forth.'

The man was in his late forties, the guard said, and had his own business, which was quite good. He was single and had no previous convictions. The explanation he gave was that he had had some drink taken and had forgotten himself on the spur of the moment.

'How do you account for this filthy behaviour?' the Justice asked the defendant.

'It wasn't premeditated,' he replied. 'It had hardly happened when I realized what had happened to myself.'

'But you must have known,' said the Justice.

'They were standing around me, you see. Two of them had their hands in my pockets,' said the man.

'That's no excuse for allowing children to do what they did to you,' said the Justice.

'I didn't ask them,' said the man.

'Do you know anything about his activities?' the justice asked the guard.

'He told me he's going steady at the moment and hopes to get married,' replied the guard.

'Hopes to get married? How old is he now?' asked the Justice, and the guard told him.

'Well, I don't know what to do with you,' the Justice said to the defendant. 'You have committed a very serious offence, apart from a filthy one. Even though these children are members of the itinerant class, you shouldn't have been a party to it. The only thing in your favour is that you have no previous convictions.'

'He seems to be very straightforward. He didn't deny it. He admitted it to me and was very cooperative,' interjected the guard.

'Were you ever under medical care? Have you ever been treated for any complaint?' asked the Justice. The man shook his head.

'Taking account of your previous good character and good employment and the fact you have no previous convictions,' remarked the Justice, 'I could send you to prison, but I'm satisfied this was an isolated case. Are you satisfied of that, guard? I will fine you five pounds, with fourteen days to pay or two months' imprisonment in default. Furthermore, you will be bound over for twelve months, and it will be a condition of the bond that you do not interfere with, molest or indecently assault children of tender years.'

'I've never done it before,' said the man.

'And you'll never do it again?' asked the Justice.

'Never again,' said the man.

'If you enter into the bond you'll hear no more about it,' said the Justice.

HAS SHE A BLACK EYE
OR ANYTHING?

THE IRISH TIMES
JULY 1974

It was hot, the court was crowded, the husband in the dock asked for a remand that he might get a solicitor, and his wife, her blackened face disguised, stood at the side near the door, glancing from her husband to District Justice Ó hUadhaigh in Dublin District Court Four.

'Has she a black eye or anything?' the Justice asked the prosecuting guard.

'I have,' said the woman.

'She has,' said the guard.

Her two eyes were blackened and there were dark bruises above and below her lips.

'What age are you?' the Justice asked her.

'I'm twenty-one,' she said.

'What age are you?' the Justice asked the husband.

'I'm twenty-five,' he said.

They both looked young. You could feel the strain.

'I won't be hearing the case,' said the Justice, who was about to go on holiday. 'Has he ever been in court before for beating his wife?'

'No,' said the guard.

'I'll remand you on an independent bail of fifty pounds over and above your husband's estate.'

'I'm a dealer,' the mother said.

'That's very nice,' said the Justice shortly. 'Where's that guard gone? There he is. The guard will take you back to your home and you may take whatever you require until the case is heard. Where will you live in the meantime?'

'With me mother,' said the young man.

'With the mammy,' the Justice said.

'There's nowhere else,' said the mother, defending her son.

'He's not going to stay with you! What do you think of that?' the Justice challenged her.

'He can't leave the country,' the mother said angrily. 'He can't leave everything behind—his van and his business and all.'

'Until this matter is settled,' the Justice stated coldly, 'in the interests of peace in the locality and the house itself, the locality more than the house, he may not go back to that area. You all live beside each other. The guard will take you home to get what you need until you come back next week with your solicitor. If you're seen around there in the meantime, and the guard brings that to the attention of this court, you'll be in breach of the bond.'

He looked at the mother. He looked at the son. The son's wife was already gone.

CONSENTING ADULTS

∞ ∞

THE IRISH TIMES
SEPTEMBER 1975

Dublin District Court Four was cleared of the public. Two men entered the dock and sat apart like strangers before District Justice Ua Donnchadha. The wife of one of the men sat in a corner at the back of the court. Solicitors for both men said they would be pleading guilty.

As the result of a complaint, the prosecuting guard said he had gone to the public toilets in a certain area. After waiting there a while, the door to one of the cubicles opened, and one man came out. The guard saw a second man still inside the cubicle.

He stopped both the accused and spoke to them outside the toilets. At that time they denied everything. Later they admitted all. The guard proposed to read their statements.

'In view of the wife's presence in court, perhaps we needn't hear statements,' one solicitor delicately suggested.

'If the wife does not wish to hear she can go outside,' the Justice said. 'This is a public court.'

The wife remained and listened to the two accounts of the men's sexual activities together in the toilet. Neither had any previous convictions.

A psychiatrist to the younger man, who was twenty-five, was called to testify. The defendant had been referred to him by a priest.

'He has been attending me regularly five days a week since this happened,' the doctor said. 'The conclusion I came to is that first he is very sincere. I am very slow to come to conclusions about cases which are pending in court. But in this case I am convinced by his sincerity. He did not think in fact that he could be treated, and was wrongly advised to this effect by a psychiatric nurse. Depending on his desire, he can be treated with psychotherapy … no medication is being used.'

'Was it fair to suggest that he was sexually immature?' the solicitor asked.

He was, the doctor agreed.

The Justice interjected to wonder why men behaved in this manner? 'It's a completely unnatural performance,' the justice said. 'Normally at his age young men are more interested in people of the opposite sex.'

There was a total pattern involving the young man's background which explained it, the doctor said. 'But he did have a girlfriend and he dreams about girls. However, he lacks self-confidence and feels inferior.'

'Would you say that he could have a fruitful relationship with a member of the opposite sex? That he could marry and have children?' the solicitor asked hopefully.

'Yes, indeed,' the doctor said.

The other solicitor went into the case history of the married man. He had married two years ago and his job entailed his being away from home very often.

'The only conclusion I can come to is that he was suffering from depression. He'd had a few drinks taken that evening … a conviction would result in the loss of his very good job. On the strength of the job he and his wife had just bought a house with heavy mortgage commitments.'

'His wife says they are happily married. She is a very nice person, obviously. So is he … I think I can assure you, Justice, that there will be no repetition of this incident.'

The Justice pointed out that their statements implied a prior association. 'They'll have to break up all such associations,' the Justice warned. 'It's extraordinary how these types seem to gravitate to each other. In other countries, I understand, this is not an offence between adult consenting males.'

'And no one actually saw them do it,' the solicitor came in.

'Well,' said the Justice firmly, 'it's against the law here. The law's the law and they broke the law. One answer is prison obviously. If they had been dealt with before a jury they could have gotten penal servitude, strange as it seems to say. In the interests of justice, I will bind them in their own bonds to keep the peace for a year.

'It goes without saying that their association must break up and there must be no repetition of this.'

ARMAGH IS A FEMINIST ISSUE

THE IRISH TIMES
JUNE 1980

There is menstrual blood on the walls of Armagh Prison in Northern Ireland. The thirty-two women on dirt strike there have not washed their bodies since 8 February 1980. They use their cells as toilets and for over two hundred days now they have lived amid their own excreta, urine, and blood.

The windows and spy holes are boarded up. Flies and slugs grow fat as they grow thin. They eat and sleep and sit in this dim, electrically lit filth, without reading materials or radio or television. They are allowed out for one hour per day, hopefully to stand in the rain. The consequences for these women under these conditions at the least will be urinary, pelvic, and skin infections. At worst they face sterility, and possible death.

They are guarded by male warders presided over by a male governor, and attended by a male doctor. Relations between the women and these men have never been very good. In an ordinary medical atmosphere, for example in a Dublin hospital, women who have depended on men for advice, consultation and treatment have often had grounds for complaint.

In the present situation of confrontation and hostility that exists in Armagh Jail, it would be fair to assume that the relationship between the women prisoners and the men charged with responsibility for them is not such as to allay anxiety about the bodily health of the women.

What business, if any, is it of ours?

The choices facing feminists on the matter of Armagh Jail are clear cut. We can ignore these women or we can express concern about them. Since the suffering of women anywhere whether self-inflicted or not, cannot be ignored by feminists, then we have a clear responsibility to respond. The issue then is the nature of our response.

We can condemn the dirt strike of these women and call on them to desist. We can deplore the consequences to these women of the dirt strike and urge that action be taken to resolve the problem. Or we can support them.

It is my belief that Armagh is a feminist issue that demands our support. I believe that the thirty-two women there have been denied the fundamental rights of women, the right to bodily integrity, and I suggest that an objective examination of the events that gave rise to the dirt strike will support this contention.

*   *   *

On 7 February 1980 by common admission there occurred a confrontation in Armagh Jail between thirty-two Republican women on the one hand and on the other upwards of forty male warders, and an unspecified number of men engaged in work within the prison. The confrontation occurred shortly after noon in the dining section, where the women prisoners were partaking of an unusually attractive meal of chicken followed by apple pie.

The women were informed by the prison governor that their cells would be searched while they stayed in the dining area. The authorities were looking for the black berets and skirts the women occasionally wore in the yard when conducting a political parade in commemoration or celebration of some Republican happening outside.

The wearing of this makeshift uniform was a symbolic rejection of the criminal status the authorities had imposed on them, and a palpable projection of the women's own self-image as political prisoners. The arguments for and against political status are well rehearsed to the initiated.

The position of Britain is, briefly, that those who commit offences against the State are criminals.The position of Republicans is, briefly, that having been charged with political offences in consequence of which they are denied the right to trial by jury and must appear before a special Diplock court, they are by definition political prisoners. In support of their case, Republicans point to the existence of political prisoners within Northern Ireland jails who were sentenced before 1 March 1976. The British case of criminalization is arbitrary, resting on the decision to abolish political status after that date.

In February of this year, the British authorities were preparing to take an even more arbitrary step. Legislation was about to be enacted which would deny retrospective political status to those who were now facing conviction for acts committed before March 1976. To that end it was presumably necessary to remove even the physical vestiges of imaginary political status. The statutory right of women prisoners in Northern Ireland to wear their own clothes was changed to an obligation to wear civilian clothes that were not of a certain colour or cut—no black berets or skirts allowed.

As a result of the confrontation in Armagh on 7 February, the women prisoners, many of whom suffered physical injury, were locked in their cells for twenty-four hours. Bodily integrity was denied them when they were refused access to toilets or a washing facility during this time. For those twenty-four hours the women, some of them menstruating, were not allowed to wash and were forced to use chamber pots for all bodily functions.

The chamber pots overflowed. The outrageous humiliation was complete. The rest is a matter of smelly and filthy history, one chapter of which testified to a calculated sexual assault upon them in the early months of the protest, insufficient numbers of sanitary towels were provided and the women were forced to wear bloody, saturated cloths.

The dimensions of their suffering, both mental and physical, and which can only be guessed at, make one cringe. These women entered jail at a young age, many of them in their teens. Given the widespread ignorance of the complex mechanism of the female body that prevails in this country, North and South, it is fair to assume that these women are less aware than they might be of what is currently happening to their bodies.

What confidence are we to have in the authorities of Armagh Jail when one considers the case of Pauline McLoughlin from Derry, as outlined in Tim Pat Coogan's book *On The Blanket* ?

Charged in October 1976, the author records, 'she spent sixteen months on remand, during which time she displayed a tendency to get sick after eating. In February 1978, she was sentenced and joined her comrades—on protest for political status. At this stage it was not certain whether Pauline would be moved to the Special Category status wing, as the offences she was sentenced for occurred before March 1976, and the withdrawal of political status. Therefore Pauline remained in the protest wing with her comrades. Her privileges were not refused pending a reply from the Northern Ireland Office, NIO. During this time Pauline's father became seriously ill, and since there was no direction from the NIO she was permitted to visit her father in hospital under escort. However, in March 1978, the NIO ruled that she was not entitled to Special Category status, Pauline immediately joined her comrades on the protest and her privileges were removed.

'She began to faint at intervals. On Monday, 18 March she was brought to the prison doctor who warned her that she was going to die, that she was inflicting the conditions on herself and she would continue to deteriorate. The prisoners say that he recorded the conversation in case any question of a law suit against him arose. She was weighed and recorded as being six stones and one pound at that time. Finally her companions persuaded her to come off the dirty protest.'

On 19 July Pauline McLoughlin was taken from the prison to an intensive care unit of a Belfast hospital, at a reported weight of five stones. After one week she was returned to prison, where her weight continues to rise and fall. What is to be done? Shall we feminists record that she is inflicting the conditions on herself in case any question of moral dereliction arises against us? The menstrual blood on the walls of Armagh prison smells to high heaven. Shall we turn our noses up?

SCHOOL WAS NEVER LIKE THIS

THE IRISH PRESS
JULY 1981

Dear Mammy,
Forget my previous letter about the West. All is changed utterly. I am like the women who discovered Smirnoff. I have discovered the Merriman Summer School. Actually, that involves quite a bit of vodka, too.

There I was in Lahinch last Friday, looking out the front window of Mary Comber's bar and asking why I should go back to school at my age. She said school was never like this and advised me to stick around. At six o'clock who should come flying along in a helicopter but Charles Haughey, our Taoiseach. He sped up the main street in a car, followed by half of Fianna Fáil. I saw Senator Treasa Honan, Senator P.J. O'Meara and Frank Dunlop whizz by. Whatever they said to each other in the Aberdeen Arms must have cheered Charlie up, because half an hour later he decided to walk back down the Main Street again and face the public.

It was like high noon. Unfortunately it was also time for high tea and he had the street to himself and nobody saw him. So I left my window and walked down after him, round the corner, and into the Lahinch Leisure Centre. There I fell into the Merriman Summer School.

Mary Comber was right. School was never like this.

The tables at the centre were loaded with whole salmon and lobsters and prawns and mackerel and salads of many kinds, and Charlie told us to eat our fill, courtesy of Bord Iascaigh Mhara, and said that joy should be unconfined. There were hundreds of people there dining like ancient Irish royalty in a most unconfined fashion and Bord Iascaigh Mhara said we could eat like this all the time if we'd only take more interest in fish.

We kept on looking out the window at the sea which was trying to crash in on top of us, and we agreed that the Bord was absolutely right. Then John de Courcy Ireland gave us a lecture on the Irish maritime tradition, and I heard things I never knew about. Did you know about the sea and the 1916 rebellion, Mammy? Neither did I, but a book has been written about it.

After the lecture, we went around all the pubs where the classes are held. Then we went back to the centre for a céilí. I met a man called Tom Hardiman who used to run RTE, and he danced the feet off me too. The Merriman School is like that.

Who is this Brian Merriman, I hear you ask? He wrote a poem in Irish over a hundred years ago. It is called 'The Midnight Court' and is all about Irish women complaining that Irish men are not nearly as sexy as they should be. When the poem was translated into English everybody was affronted and said it should be banned, and so it was, and then it was resurrected again in 1968, and the people who resurrected it decided to show that things had changed, and that Irish women and Irish men could have a grand old time together if they put their minds to it. And also they could speak Irish while doing so, and dance and drink and learn things together, and turn day into night and night into day if they felt like it.

Everybody feels like it. I have seen sights this weekend, Mammy. I saw a man called Senator Shane Ross being taken on a crash course in Irish culture by a man called Senator John A. Murphy. They went to the céilí too on Friday night, and set off for Kinvara on Saturday to see a convention of hookers.

Hookers are boats.

On Sunday they went to Béal na Bláth. At least, they were supposed to go, but Senator Ross got interested in the classes and stayed behind.

I met a man called Joey Murrin, who is very enthusiastic about fishing. He came down from Killybegs with a load of crab claws in the boot of his car, and Bord Iascaigh Mhara cooked them and we ate them, and Joey gave us a lecture on the Irish fishing industry.

The sea is swimming with fish, Mammy. One modern boat can bring in enough mackerel in one trip to feed two million Irish people. A man called Arthur Reynolds told us that. And if we don't want to eat that many mackerel we can sell them abroad and bring down the balance of payments.

Another man called Eamon Gallagher who is the European Director General of Fisheries got all cross with Joey, and Arthur and said if we caught too many fish there would be none left and we have to leave them time to breed. He wants to draw up rules and have everybody follow his rules, but Joey and Arthur said he must be codding and that we have to fight for Irish fish in Irish waters for the Irish people, and that the rule should be applied to the ocean beyond our territorial limits.

On Sunday morning I went to a poetry reading. That's right. I got up in the morning, and me on me holidays. This school wants to make you do things. We all rushed over to Ennistymon and heard ancient Irish poems about the seas, and the fish and the fishermen. The fishermen have sayings about the weather that I found very interesting. It comes from a book called *An tOileánach*. The fishermen say that when times are really stormy you would keep your head in, like 'a rabbit in a burrow in Innisvickillaune.' After the poetry reading we rushed into hotels and pubs for more classes and a little drink because, as Ciaran Mac Mathuna puts it, poetry reading is thirsty work.

I have to finish this letter now, Mammy, and get ready for another céilí tonight. But first I have to go to my classes in the pub, and then on to another lecture about the folklore of the sea by Dr Seamus O Catháin of UCD. I missed Justin Keating's lecture about the importance of the sea on Saturday night because my class got all involved in a debate about whether Joey Murrin or Eamon Gallagher was right about fishing stocks and one drink borrowed another, and before we knew it it was four o'clock in the morning. Or was it five?

The school ends this Thursday and I will try to come back then, but I don't know, because Bill Loughnane is getting married next Saturday and they say the crack will be only terrific. I met an old man who has shaved himself in preparation for the evening. He says Bill's forthcoming marriage has raised his own prospects no end and he showed me a photograph of Bill and his intended and said 'Mother of God tonight, what do you think of that?'

So I'll try and get home before September, but I really don't know. As far as I can see, if you sit in the front window of Mary Comber's bar in Lahinch the whole world will come to your doorstep. Did I tell you Dick Burke was here on last Friday night? I wish I had read 'The Midnight Court' when I first went to school. Education is such fun.

Mise le meas
Nell

THE ACCUSING FINGER OF
A DERRY SUPERGRASS

MAGILL
APRIL 1983

Magistrate John Fyffe said dispassionately, 'If there is any disruption by any member of the public, or any relative—any person guilty of disruption or harassment will be excluded from the court.' He sat back and the door in the wall to his right opened. Three men in civilian clothes came out and down, quickly and smoothly, and were in place below the magistrate within seconds. The third man was Raymond Gilmour.

He could not easily be seen from the body of the court. He sat in the chair in the witness box, effectively at ground level, while two civilians, members of the RUC Special Branch, stood shoulder to shoulder with their backs against the box, staring out and up into the body of the courtroom. The twenty-eight prisoners in the raised dock with their relatives packed into benches, like seats in a football stand, were faced with a human curtain.

Raymond Gilmour did not look like Raymond Gilmour. As lately as twelve months ago he looked just like the prisoners in the dock, the young men and women from the Bogside and the Creggan among whom he had grown up, with many of whom he had socialized, and with one of whom he had been drinking on the night before the police came to his Creggan home, and loaded him and his wife and children into an armoured car and their furniture into a removal lorry, and took them into 'protective custody.' Later that morning they returned to Creggan and took away the man with whom Gilmour had been drinking, charged him with a great many things, and charged a great many other people as well.

That man and the others in the dock looked like they always looked—and Raymond Gilmour used to look too— like part of a working-class crowd in T-shirts and plain sweaters and plain haircuts, with pale faces or a ruddy complexion, the odd tattoo, and scuffed shoes occasionally visible when they leaned back and rested a foot on dock.

Fully visible to the press alone, Raymond Gilmour was beautifully dressed in a tailored, slim-line, dark blue suit. His shirt was gleaming white; the striped silver and dark red tie a little too glittering. His skin was tanned, the black beard trimmed neatly. His hair was glossy, parted but blow-dried so that it fell gently either side. He looked, as they say in Derry, a credit.

He sat concealed, and did not look up into the public gallery where his mother and three sisters and brother sat. His father had been taken into custody by the Provisional IRA after Gilmour turned informer, and the IRA have said they will kill him if Raymond Gilmour does not retract.

On Monday morning 25 July at twenty minutes past eleven, he started to give evidence. For one hour he spoke, but not in a rush and not in an unbroken flow. First the prosecution, taking his cue from a very thick dossier of Gilmour's statements that looked like an unbound novel, asked a question. 'On the afternoon of … were you … ,' and as he spoke a woman seated below the magistrate typed. If she did not get the question she asked the prosecutor to repeat it and he did, then she read it back. Raymond Gilmour answered and the woman typed and sometimes she'd ask him to repeat a phrase.

If you came from Derry, his halting evidence was like a gentle journey round the town. First he went to Hugh Duffy's house in Lislane Drive—of course, you mentally nod, that's Hugh over there, know that street, know his mother, a widow who worked as a cleaner. What's she doing now, you wonder. Then Raymond says Hugh sent him to Ducksie Doherty and instinctively your head nods in greeting, grand nickname, terrific smile Ducksie, all teeth. And then Raymond ended up in McCann's fish and chipper in the Brandywell.

McCann's, a location to conjure with, the place where you go after bingo, or a dance in the Lourdes Community Hall, its glass window comfortingly lit up in winter. Then Raymond mentions a street in the Brandywell, not familiar, where Raymond was shown how to use the rifle. The Brandywell is being reconstructed with new housing everywhere, and as you puzzle this one you are jerked back to the courtroom.

The rifle was hidden under a concrete block. 'There was a green tile over the block, lino over the tile, and the cooker was on top of that, Gilmour explained as he named the man and women in that house. There was frosted glass, so no one could see through it. It could be true, it might not be true. 'Sorry, your honour,' he says conversationally, 'I forgot to mention Cathy Miller and Betty McSheffrey.'

A defence solicitor comes to his feet and says that he cannot hear the witness or see him either. The same solicitor had made the point two weeks previously about Michael Quigley, another Derryman who also informed on Derrymen, many of whom were now in the dock, accused by Gilmour. On that occasion Magistrate John Petrie disallowed the plea, and Quigley remained hidden behind Special Branch 'minders,' for 'reasons of security.'

Quigley, fully visible only to the press, had kept his eyes trained on a spot below the magistrate, and unfolded his arms four times in six hours. His face had been immobile as an identikit picture.

Gilmour was not under cross examination and sat forward when the solicitor protested and looked at the solicitor so that everybody could see the witness clearly. He was talking again, his face turned back to the magistrate, so it is certain that he did not see his mother stand.

Martin McGuinness, Sinn Féin member for Derry, earlier escorted Mrs Gilmour to a seat which afforded a central view of her son, whom she had not seen for twelve months. Everybody else, including her other son and three daughters, was herded into a section behind the witness box. The RUC had been posted one to each end of the vacant rows like recalcitrant theatre goers refusing to let people pass once the show has started. McGuinness and Mrs Gilmour were marooned in a sea of green uniforms.

She rose now as her son spoke, stepping past McGuinness and the police, and then left for the exit. Her son was gazing at a spot below the magistrate's bench. She was gazing at the door.

'Raymond, she called softly over her shoulder, but not looking, 'Raymond, son, you know I'm here. I can't listen any more to you saying them things about your friends.'

Her head drooped, but as the door opened before her, he was on his way without a glance to his own door accompanied by his minders, the three men moving in perfect unison, and Raymond Gilmour was gone in perfect tandem with his mother, in an opposite direction.

The silence, brief though it was, was heartstopping. Then Raymond Gilmour's sister stood up.

'Your honour, can my mother not speak to Raymond? She hasn't seen him for a year.' The police moved quickly to her.

'Your honour,' she repeated, clearly and not shouting. The police were on top of her, grabbing her and pushing her, and she shouted and one of them lifted her off the bench and stumbled down the aisle, and she was pulling the policeman's hair, and her splayed body was blocking the doorway, but reinforcements punched her through.

The second sister was on her feet, pleading that her younger sister be left alone, and even as she shouted the RUC were descending on her from both sides, not able to grab her body because she was in the middle of the row, but her arms were tugged out on either side like a crucifixion without a cross or nails and she was pulled head first over the benches and over the head of the third sister who had risen to her feet, and was trying to stop the passage of her sister's body, but she was also grabbed and the two were lost in a melée of green uniforms.

John Gilmour, the eldest boy, meanwhile rose to his feet. His mouth was wide open, but no sound came from it. His fists were clenched, his whole frame was strain-ing, but he did not move because if he moved he would be removed and there would be no family member present to call Ray-mond home. The court was suddenly quiet again, the sisters gone, but he was on his feet, agony in his features. The RUC gathered below him, not touching.

'What are you looking at? I'm not doing anything, I'm not saying anything,' he said, trembling from the strain of saying nothing. We all, magistrate, press, defendants, rela-tives, special branch, prison guards, gazed frozen upon this spectacle. John Gilmour looked like a man at bay, a rabbit in headlights. The doors swung open again and the screams of his sisters and knockabout noises came from the pas-sage.

There issued from his mouth a long bellow, and as it came he launched himself into the scrum. They passed him to the aisle but he regained his feet there and stood resisting the downward pull, and seven policemen, two on his knees, two around his waist, two on his arms, and one behind him pulling his neck back. They tumbled, punching each other down the stairs and out the door.

All the Gilmours were gone.

* * *

Proud Derry memories of civil-rights resistance went with them. A few shouts from the gallery and dock, a few bodies jerked, a few faces streaming with silent tears marked their passing, but no one had gone to their help.

If the court had been emptied, Raymond Gilmour would have been under no pressure giving evidence. The Republican prisoners have been instructed to hold themselves in check and suffer indignity that they might remain to pressurize Raymond Gilmour.

The press, too, is trained to go against human nature and stand aside in the interests of maintaining the written record. The court resumed amid the silence. The door in the wall opened and the two minders and Gilmour flowed down to resume positions. He did not look up into the gallery. He took up at once, without prompting, where he had left off, and the typewriter went clack-clack, and the sun shone in through the windows. It was as though the waters had heaved and erupted and then closed calmly again over some monstrous thing.

Raymond Gilmour was in the High Flats in the Bogside now, trying to plant a bomb beside the British Army lookout post on the roof. He pretended to court a female member of the unit in the stairwell while keeping an eye out for the troops. The others came back to report that the trapdoor into the roof was beyond their reach. They dispatched a man to the nearby Rocking Chair bar, run cooperatively by ex-felons, for a tall stool. The stool arrived, was mounted, and the bomb was planted. They retired from the eighth floor to a flat on the fifth and waited. They waited for hours. It did not go off. Back up to the bar for the stool, back up onto the roof for the bomb, recover it, and away to their various homes. It was almost funny, if it wasn't so serious.

That part of the evidence was now concluded, the prosecution said, and he must now ask Raymond Gilmour to identify the people he had named, if they were present in court. His minders drew aside like a curtain, and Raymond Gilmour turned to face the people he had grown up with. If the magistrate were to believe his evidence, and return them for trial, and they were convicted, they would go to jail for life for murder or fifteen years, or ten years, or five years if the charge was relatively minor, like membership of the IRA.

He would have to point them out, point his finger. 'That man there,' he said, 'the man on the left, with the yellow T-shirt ... that girl between the policemen.' One man would not wait. 'Is it me you're looking for, Gilmour?' 'Yes, that's you,' Gilmour replied, then moved to the next.

And then there was the young man he could not find at all. Finally he smiled as in fond remembrance, and some prisoners turned smiles on the man he finally loc-ated, because this man was quite small and his size was the butt of fond jokes.

The communal link snapped as another prisoner rose to his feel and snarled in fury,

'Gilmour, you yellow bastard!' and the prison guards were onto him, but he had already turned to go down below, because he knew the procedure.

'I hope your da gets stiffed!' he yelled, and this time the prison guards pushed him.

A clatter of feet, a muffled call, and the waters closed again, and Raymond Gilmour continued to point at people. The court rose for lunch.

On the road outside, Mrs Gilmour, surrounded by her three daughters and son John, stood waiting, 'I'm sorry,' she said to everyone. 'I just couldn't bear it.' The plan had been for her to say, 'Raymond, can you identify me?' That would have brought him to his senses, for was he not brainwashed, couldn't everybody see that her son had been programmed by the police?

She stood in the roadway pleading; some relatives of the prisoners moved stiffly past her. The Gilmour family have not disowned Raymond, have they? But if they did, he'd be beyond all emotional bidding. He doesn't care about his father, he did not break down even when his wife and children left him and returned to the Creggan.

But look what his wife said about the time he tried to kill himself in that hotel in Cyprus, overdosing on her tranquillizers. Didn't she say he was drinking heavily?

'He rang me on Mother's Day,' Mrs Gilmour said. He rang every member of his family, Martin McGuinness confirmed, and seemed incoherent, saying he'd be killed if he returned to Derry.

'Then he wrote me a letter thanking me for rearing him,' said Mrs Gilmour, 'but I didn't rear him for this, did I, Martin?' She turned for consolation to the two representatives of Sinn Féin, Mc-Guinness and Mitchell McLaughlin, who have become her own minders.

How come she never noticed, some relatives wondered as they left her on the road, crying? Hasn't the prosecution confirmed to the defence solicitors that Raymond Gilmour was a paid police teenage tout long before he joined the IRA?

He was a tout when he joined the IRA 'to avenge the death of my best friend Colm McNutt, shot by the soldiers.' Who set McNutt up, relatives ask? McNutt tried to hijack a car in the Bogside, and the four occupants, members of the SAS in civilian dress, shot him dead. It takes time to set up a hijacking and he would have had to tell his unit beforehand.

'That woman there', Mrs Gilmour indicated a woman who had frozen her with a glance 'is very cold to me.'

'You have to understand her feelings, mammy,' a daughter explained, 'her man might be jailed for years and she has a family to raise.'

'But it's not my fault,' Mrs Gilmour burst. 'My man's gone too.' Her Sinn Féin minders consoled her. For months they have defended her against the outrage of the community. Gilmour's returned wife Lorraine had already been thumped by the wife of a prisoner as she sat in a Derry café. Martin McGuinness had gone to the wife to explain that this was not good. Taking tea in Derry, living it up in a Cyprus hotel while my husband is in jail, the wife had spluttered.

The Gilmour family has to be protected, Sinn Féin explains. They are the emotional link with Raymond and if that link is broken there's no hope of him recanting. Some of the prisoners' relatives are insisting Raymond Gilmour's father be shot dead. Punish Raymond, punish the Gilmours, punish somebody for what's being done.

There are fewer jokes around Derry about how the sixty-two year-old father is having the time of his life in Donegal in the company of the lads. Fewer jokes about how it does a man good to get away from the wife. If Mr Gilmour is shot now, goes the reasoning, it will only stiffen Raymond's resolve. There is a point, though, to shooting him dead anyway, as a warning to other informers, unless the Gilmour family can draw Raymond back. The Gilmour family, isolated, draws emotional sustenance from Sinn Féin, because they live in dread of what the Provisional IRA will do. This deadly scenario has become a commonplace of casual discussion in Derry.

No one has come to Gilmour's defence. Officially he's doing what the Roman Catholic Bishop of Derry and the SDLP have called for—giving information about killings —but neither the Bishop nor the SDLP has defended his stance. This has not gone unnoticed. The mental savagery of the Belfast courtroom has seeped into the streets of Derry.

People are informing against Raymond Gilmour and Michael Quigley now. Word went out that the defence solicitors needed to know everything there was to know about them along the lines of character assassination, and information came back in abundance. The kitchen sink was thrown at Quigley. Weren't you in the remedial class at school?

Quigley's parents, still living in Derry, have to live with this exposé of their son. The Gilmours are being prepared for similar and 'worse revelations' about Raymond. Information is flowing in and spilling over. It is almost merciful that the Gilmours have been thrown out of court and will not be there. It might take weeks to persuade the magistrate to let them back in, the solicitors informed the family that Monday. The forlorn little bunch, beaten by the police, ignored by Raymond and by some prisoners and relatives, ignorant of their father's fate, trailed off to the cars for the journey home.

The rest of Derry moved up to a Portakabin on a concrete base, surrounded by protective fencing and pitched in the middle of a wasteland opposite Crumlin Road Jail. Inside the cabin, decorated and clean and muggy with warmth, children played with toys. The cabin and its staff of volunteers was set up by an international children's organization. People can leave their children there while they visit relatives in jail or call in for tea or soup and biscuits while awaiting developments. The staff were wonderful

How had those relatives who did not resent the Gilmours maintained composure while the RUC assaulted that family? 'You think of policemen being killed by the IRA some day, somewhere. You keep that in your mind while you sit absolutely still and you're not sorry at the prospect.' This from a mild Derrywoman sitting in a Belfast wasteland, who normally spends summer days with her family on a Donegal beach.

Conversation turns from the RUC to court room procedure. The solicitors want to save cross examination until the formal trial next year. There's no point giving Raymond Gilmour a dry run now they argue, you're just giving the police time to prepare him. You can be sure they've broken him already. Why give them more time? Throw stuff at him while he's vulnerable.

But is he vulnerable, they wonder? This is not the Gilmour some knew. Is that how they brainwashed in Korea, in Vietnam? Never mind, you wouldn't find in-formers tolerated in an English system.

One woman present has one son in the dock and another a solicitor in the defence counsel. The son in the dock is not allowed to sit beside his wife of eighteen months, also charged. She got bail because she was pregnant. The child has since been born. If he is convicted of the killing of which he has been accused, her childbearing years will be over by the time he gets out, assuming her body is not destroyed in Armagh Jail where she might be sent if Gilmour is believed. The young woman's mother keeps vigil in court from her wheelchair.

Lunch was over and they trooped back to listen, disbelievingly, while Raymond Gilmour continued to in-form. Fifty-five more people will face his accusations when this lot is done with. How could he do it, they kept asking. How could Quigley have done it? Quigley had already provided his own answer. He was not an informer, he told his cross-questioner. He was a converted terrorist. When had he converted, the defence asked.

'On the road to Castlereagh,' he said, his immobile face an identikit mask.

REFERENDUM, PART ONE

IN DUBLIN
APRIL 1983

s predicted in the last issue, though only in jest, a strange thing has come to pass—Michael Keating of Fine Gael has earnestly advocated that a referendum be held to decide which form of wording the people want in the referendum. Depending on the vote, the preferred wording will be put to the people in a second referendum; and they can then vote once more on whether they ever wanted it in the Constitution in the first place.

Alternately, both forms of words can be put directly to the Dáil on 20 April 1983. If the Fianna Fáil wording succeeds, it will be put to the Senate, where a rigidly disciplined Fine Gael majority will defeat it. It will then return to the Dáil, where they will have to consider changing it to ensure passage back up to the Senate. The changed wording would probably resemble the current second Fine Gael form of wording. Why not settle for that version right now?

Fianna Fáil can't accept that wording right now because it would leave the matter to be decided by the Dáil, and TDs may make decisions without reference to the people or courts, says Charlie Haughey. They might introduce abortion the very next day, he said on RTE radio.

Fine Gael cannot accept the Fianna Fáil wording now or at any time because it would leave the issue of abortion to be decided by the courts and the courts might make a decision without reference to the people or the Dáil. The courts might introduce abortion the very next day, says Fine Gael.

The Responsible Society, a constituent association of PLAC, says we must not grow fatigued and give up on the proposed referendum because abortion may be introduced without recourse to the courts or the consent of TDs without some form of words. It might be brought in by some TD in whom the balance of power in a hung Dáil is vested and to whom the prize of legalized abortion is held out as a carrot by some power-hungry would-be Taoiseach.

Dr Julia Vaughan, the chairwoman of the Pro-Life Amendment Campaign (PLAC), got to the heart of the matter when she said there's no point 'closing the stable door after the horse has bolted.' Naturally, by 'horse' she meant woman. Alarmed, like the forward line of the Irish Rugby Team, they scrummed immediately in a city centre church at midnight and lit candles during a three-hour vigil. They were 'atoning for abortion' and 'spiritually adopting' babies that are not yet even a glint in a man's eye, praying that God protect these future babies from the ravaging intent of some slaughterhouse momma,

PLAC are now considering a campaign against the amendment, if the FG amendment gets through the Dáil, and steps are in train to change their initials from PLAC to PLACAFGA. The Society for the Protection of the Unborn is ready to call themselves SPUC for FFA and Against the FGA or SPUCFFAAFGA for short. Fine Gael is ready to campaign against the FF wording, if it gets through, under the handy title FGAFFA and Also Against Abortion or FGAFFAAAA, while Fianna Fáil is ready to campaign against Fine Gael wording using the title FFAFGAAAA.

The nation is faced with the prospect of going to the polls some day while muttering various mantras to ensure that the correct vote is cast for the correct stand. 'I'm FFA-

GAAAA, what are you? You're a FGAFAAAA? Aaagh, get away from me you dirty git.' The whole matter is as clear as daylight to the various religious groupings in Ireland. The Roman Catholic Church supports the Fianna Fáil wording. The major Protestant Churches will support the Fine Gael wording if they have to, though they'd prefer no amendment at all.

Like the Irish Rugby Team, Cardinal Tomas O Fiaich has suddenly been caught up in the urgency of it all. He revealed that the number of unborn Irish babies killed in any single year through abortions in England far outnumbers the total number of already-born Irish and British citizens killed in Northern Ireland in any year since the current war began. The Cardinal has not been paying enough attention to John Devine of the *Sunday Independent*, who revealed last year that a British soldier had just been killed in an IRA 'post-abortion' operation.

Now known as the AAC, the Anti-Amendment Campaign has pursued a pristine path of clarity through this muddle, but events have conspired to force them to consider a name-change. They are campaigning against any amendment at all, no matter what the words say, or AAAAAC in short. By now, people are asking quietly what in God's name this is all about? It used to be that one could crisply say, 'This is not about abortion. It's about the best means to ensure that abortion would never be introduced for any reason or exception in this country.'

Unfortunately, both forms of wording meant one had to explain that various exceptions would flow from either form. Under the Fianna Fáil form, abortion in certain circumstances might be introduced through a new Dáil law—not to mention all the problems either form raised about contraception by implicitly referring to it or ignoring it.

GOLDEN BALLS

∞ ∞

IN DUBLIN
JUNE 1983

The teenage son of a Fianna Fáil TD has taken to hanging around the Dáil bar handing out pairs of feet to whomsoever takes his fancy. The tiny gold-played feet, mounted on a pin, are replicas in shape and size of the feet of a foetus. Those who pin these feet to their lapels are declaring to the world their love of the foetus, their opposition to abortion and their desire that human sexuality should be so regulated that no women would ever be caught in what Nuala Fennell called 'the unremitting nightmare of an unwanted pregnancy.'

It's sweet, really, to see men wear feet in their lapels, thus acknowledging their function in the creation of pregnancy. Unfortunately though, feet means foetus, hence pregnancy, and what women would prefer is the absence of any feet in the womb without their prior consent.

Is there any other method by which men could signal their desire that every pair of feet should be a wanted pair? Is there any other method by which men could signal to the world their determination to play a responsible role in the matter of reproduction? They love their badges: their lapels are covered in them. Given that men can't donate blood, foreswear drink, follow a football team, speak Irish or kill other men without some decoration across their chests announcing it, could there be designed a more apt symbol of their responsible conduct in affairs sexual?

There could.

I have designed one myself.

I put it forward for your consideration, dear reader.

Men should be allowed to wear a pair of golden balls in their lapels. These balls would signify that the wearer declines unprotected sexual intercourse with females of childbearing age.

This plan has many and exciting possibilities.

All males, as soon as they have reached the age of puberty, will qualify for a pair of golden balls. Before presentation of the balls they will naturally have to undergo a simple sex education course in which they will be instructed on such matters as sperm count, menstruation, zygotes, implantation, nappy-washing, the four am feed, the length of the Dublin Corporation housing list and the factors influencing repayment of our foreign borrowings which in turn influences our ability to feed all comers.

Each pair of balls will be stamped with a serial number indicating the name, address and fingerprints of the recipient. Any male found without a pair of balls will be required to give an account of his movements to a ban garda. Any male proposing sexual intercourse with a woman shall be required to hand his balls into her safe keeping until such time as her period has arrived or the baby is born, in which latter case possession of the male's balls by the woman shall be proof of paternity.

This might seem a repressive manner in which to treat balls, but these rules should only be regarded as ultimate safeguards against the cad who let the club down. What is important is the spirit of the thing. Handled properly, the balls should herald a new dawning in the area of psychosexual social relations between men and women. Men could have fun with their balls. They could even be proud of them. They could even have healthily competitive games with them. For example, the longer a man wears his balls in his lapel, the more he will be regarded as deserving of social respect. Men like to be respected. But how can we tell by looking at his balls how long he has been behaving himself?

Simple.

The more he refrains from unprotected sexual intercourse, the bigger the pair of balls he will receive. A new and bigger and better pair of balls will be issued for every year of service to the female community. Does a man lose his balls when he has fathered a wanted child? Temporarily, but for the duration of the pregnancy a nappy, tastefully reproduced in silver, will be issued. The nappy may be worn above the balls upon completion of the pregnancy and live birth, and the return, of course, of the balls by the mother to the father in question.

Will a man lose his balls if he is responsible for an unwanted pregnancy?

Yes.

To return to the yearly issue of bigger and better balls. Might this pose weighty problems for men who never betray the code of honour? Might it even, for example, introduce an element of sectarianism? Consider ministers of the cloth—of all the cloths—currently wearing manageable pairs of feet. Some of these ministers do engage in unprotected sexual intercourse, where the act is open to the transmission of life, and do so with the full blessing of their churches. Protestant ministers, to take a random example, and Jewish rabbis, marry and have children, usually in that order.

Will they be inadvertently obliged to go through life wearing smaller balls than other men of the cloth, Roman Catholics for example, whose Church absolutely prohibits them from fathering children? A Pope's balls, for example, would be of such size as to command separate transport facilities when he wings around the world.

110

Perhaps non-Catholic ministers could be issued with ruby-encrusted nappies. Incidentally, the perennial problem facing Popes—about what gift to give to whom on their travels—would be solved. Could anything more signify the Vatican's desire for and commitment to, responsible social sexuality than generous distribution of miniature reproductions of the Papal Balls?

A slogan to launch this campaign is necessary.

'Every pair of balls a wanted pair of balls.'

Revenues from the smash hit movie *The Man with the Golden Balls* should pay the costs of whatever referendum is necessary to give constitutional weight to the matter.

Balls are better than feet any old day of the week.

LONELY DEATH OF A
PREGNANT SCHOOLGIRL

∞∞∞∞∞∞∞∞∞∞∞∞∞∞∞∞∞∞∞∞∞∞

IN DUBLIN
FEBRUARY 1984

As in her pregnancy, so it was in her death. The people of Granard say in one voice, 'Ask her family.' Ann Lovett's welfare was the inviolate responsibility of her parents. Had she or they asked outsiders for help, it would have been forthcoming. The family kept silent and the community honoured the unwritten code of non-interference with the basic unit of society.

'Even if I had noticed she was pregnant,' says Canon Gilfillen, parish priest, 'I could hardly just come out and say 'You're pregnant,' could I?' A businessman who once worked with the Saint Vincent de Paul says, 'Why do you think I left Saint Vincent's? The days when you could intervene are long gone. If a family doesn't want you to acknowledge that you know, there's nothing you can do. We knew Ann Lovett was pregnant. The family said nothing. If a family's broke these days, you can't just offer them money. You can leave it secretly on the doorstep, but you can't go near them unless they ask.'

Diarmuid Lovett, father of nine and on the dole, is not broke or entirely without standing. He has lived three years in Granard above his non-trading pub, the Copper Pot. He comes from a family of substance, the Lovetts, who used to run a family building firm in nearby Kilnaleck.

His brother John owns the Copper Kettle pub in Kilnaleck. Diarmuid Lovett is of sufficient standing in the area for his daughter's death to warrant a wreath from Kilnaleck Fianna Fáil Cumann, and the attendance at her funeral of Mr John Wilson, Fianna Fáil TD, from neighbouring Mullaghoran. Diarmuid Lovett is by general reckoning an abrupt, independent man. And people could hardly just come out and offer help that might be misinterpreted as interference. It was assumed that the family knew and had made arrangements. Did the family know? 'Ask the family,' says the community, leaving the Lovetts to cope full-frontally with the disaster. The twenty-two year old sister of Ann Lovett, with whom Ann spent some time in Dublin before Christmas says, 'No comment.' The uncle of Ann Lovett says, 'Ask the family,' adding that it is the business of no one but her parents.

The family sit behind the closed doors of their pub. Diarmuid and Patricia Lovett refuse to speak to reporters. The community will not and cannot speak on their behalf. Canon Gilfillen says, 'I'd like to be able to help the family, but they've shut themselves away and seem to want to be alone. One's instinct is not to intrude.'

Ten days after Ann's death, the gardaí had not been able to secure an interview with her parents. Time is on their side, though, and they're playing a gentle waiting game. Soon, the guards know—as the townspeople know, as the public knows, as the Church knows, as the government, which has instigated a private inquiry via the Departments of Health and Education know—the parents must supply at least part of the answer. The death in a public place of a teenage girl and her newborn baby demands an attempt at explanation.

It will not be anything other than an ordeal for her parents and family. The townspeople cannot or will not help them bear that ordeal. It will be up to the family to explain how it could be that their daughter died unaided and alone. The efforts of the townspeople are directed towards explaining how they could not come to her aid, although her condition was common knowledge.

More effort has been expended in defending the social superstructure than in defending the basic unit. The Convent of Mercy School, for example, called in a solicitor who, over a period of several hours, helped them draft a statement to the effect that the staff 'did not know' that Ann Lovett was pregnant. Did they, however, 'suspect' that she was? A spokeswoman, trembling and refusing to give her name, told *In Dublin* that the school would not comment on whether or not they suspected. They certainly 'did not know.'

Nor would the school comment on the allegation that a teacher who could not stomach the nice legal distinction between 'knowing' and 'suspecting' refused to stand with the staff when a school statement was read out to news programme *Today, Tonight*.

If the school, under the authority of headmistress Sister Maria, did not know or suspect anything, did the convent, a separate institution on the same grounds under the authority of Sister Immaculata, know or suspect that Ann Lovett was pregnant? Convent sisters act as social workers in the town when they're not acting as teachers. 'No comment,' they say. Did convent teachers, in their capacity as convent sisters, approach the parents? 'No comment.'

Eventually, with or without a solicitor's help, the school and convent will make a comment to their employers, the Department of Education. In the meantime, ask the family.

While the family waits alone for the inquisitional noose to tighten, while they wait for us who are not family to tighten it, the gardaí pursue a duty which they describe as 'sickening'. A technical sexual offence has been committed, that of carnal knowledge with an under-age girl. They must interview the boyfriend with whom she had been keeping company for two years until the relationship ended a month before she gave birth. His father is dead and his mother went to England last year. The boyfriend, 'Buddy,' lives in the family house, but he was in England during the summer. Did his summer begin in May just before the pregnancy began, or later? Certainly, the gardaí know, he gave the key of his house to another youth who has left town since Ann Lovett died. Ann used to be seen coming out of that house. It would be a mercy to establish the line of paternity from there, whether or not prosecution ensues, because that would eliminate a third line of enquiry in a town bursting with outspoken rumour.

*   *   *

Since Ann Lovett's death, 'Buddy' has been visiting the grotto where she gave birth on the moss-covered stone. By night he is to be found with other youths in the pool halls or pubs, for youth does not stay at home. One such night, eleven nights after Ann Lovett's death, he stood in a pub with four of his pals, watching *The Late Late Show*. Gay Byrne was discussing pornography with an American woman of stout build. Her physical appearance drew the scorn of the youths.

Byrne ended the night by reviewing early editions of the weekend papers. The camera closed in on the semi-naked front-page woman in *The Sunday World*. 'I wouldn't mind having her,' said one of Buddy's friends, and the others groaned assent.

A studio guest criticized Mr Byrne for holding up *The Sunday World*. He replied that he was only reviewing the papers. She said the campaign against pornography was hopeless when such papers could be casually held up on view. 'She's right', said one of the youths. They attempted a discussion of this point and couldn't sustain it. *The Sunday World* couldn't be pornographic if it was a family paper. Buddy said nothing. The five boys went on to drink a little too much.

The conversation became raunchy. 'So I asked this girl to dance and held my cock right against her, like this', the eldest boy demonstrated with body movements, 'and afterwards she looked me right in the eye, said thanks, and walked off the floor, the prick-teaser.' The boys admired her cool cheek and regretted his bad luck. The discussion moved on to drink and which pint was the best brand. It was typical Saturday night peer-group conversation among young males. The youths made no connection between sexual activity and family consequences. 'Family' means married people, females and their babies.

Next morning during the Mass, Canon Gilfillen lashed out at the media for 'descending like locusts' to 'plague' and 'torment' the townspeople about a 'family matter.' His sermon veered from a plea that it should be treated as such to a tirade against men committing adultery in their hearts when they lust after women. And, he added, 'when divorce comes to the vote, as it surely will, we'll know where we stand. Against it, with the Church and with Christ.'

For his teenage parishioners, a notice cut out of an *Irish Press* article on Anne Lovett's death has been tacked high up in a corner of the bulletin board in the church porch.

'Where to find help,' the newsprint reads. 'In pregnancy' has been pencilled in. They can find help anywhere but Granard, though Ally, Cherish and Cura are in Dublin, Kilkenny, Cork, Galway, Limerick, Waterford and Sligo. No confidential telephone number in the town has been pencilled in.

Some of the services advertised use answering devices

which advise the caller to ring back. The services keep school hours. How often can you ring back from Granard's only public phone, in Main Street, when you should be in school, without attracting attention?

But then, Ann Lovett had attracted a lot of attention in her short lifetime.

'Wake up Granard!' she used shout down Main Street after nightfall. Her father used publicly to pull her home from the grocery-cum-billiard hall where she spent much of her time. The sight of him with her whom they knew to be pregnant, allayed concern as to who was taking responsibility for her welfare. 'He'd give her a cuff. Many a father does. You don't go calling the ISPCC, do you? If anything, you'd say he was doing his best, wouldn't you? And he'd be entitled to give you a cuff yourself if you stepped in. But why would we step in?'

The family looked all right. Ann Lovett looked properly fed and dressed and bright eyed. The fact that she was pregnant besides was no reason for intervention. If there was a tension between her and her father, and there was, and if it was known, which it was, and if she spent a lot of time in the houses of her friends, what else could you expect in the circumstances? It was only natural, wasn't it? That same Sunday night in a pub in the town, a group of middle-aged couples had a relaxing drink. The barman produced a leaflet which occasioned laughter. 'Prick of the Week' read the legend under a pen-and-ink reproduction of a tumescent penis, complete with scrotum. 'Prick of the Week, for having made a balls-up, is … ' read the mock certificate. It is up to the drinkers to fill in the name and the *faux pas* in question if they wish to engage in the pub joke.

A clear distinction was made between the joke and the tragedy of Ann Lovett, the mention of whose name brought an angrily defensive response. That was serious. This was funny. References to men and their sexuality is a joke, isn't

117

it? Not to be connected with women, for Christ's sake. Just like the joke on last night's *Late Late Show* about children in nappies and the connection with pornography. Naked little boys and girls aren't the same as naked big boys and girls. Can we not make jokes, for Christ's sake? Gay Byrne has a sense of humour. They identify more with television than with Church.

On Monday, thirteen days after Ann Lovett's death, the spotlight swivelled on to another institution. The guards were meeting in the station to coordinate procedure. Had a teenage boy been found dying, from whatever cause, no-one would have baulked at an enquiry. You don't walk away from a male youth, found dying in a grotto that celebrates the Virgin Birth. Nor can the guards treat maternal death as an occurrence that is as natural or miraculous as conception, pregnancy and birth.

In the event and in the panic, the other social units did. On the day of Ann Lovett's death nobody informed the guards of the events in the grotto. One of them, coming on duty at six in the evening, remarked that there were rumours in the town of an abortion. It was eight o'clock, three and a half hours after Ann Lovett had been found, before the guards established the facts, by dint of foot-slogging and telephone calls around the locality.

Doctor Tom Donohoe, the Deputy Coroner for the area, was a man well versed in the legal procedures that flow from the discovery of a dead body. It must not be moved. Doctor Donohoe, who had treated Ann Lovett for shingles on her back shortly before Christmas, treated her as she lay dying in the grotto. She was then moved by ambulance to Meath, out of the jurisdiction of Longford. The baby, which was dead and should not have been moved, was taken with her. Dr Donohoe refused to comment on what was being treated as a family affair.

Contrary to press reports, the grotto where Ann Lovett

gave birth—where her baby died, where the priest gave her Extreme Unction and baptized the baby, where the doctor treated her and her parents were brought to be with her—is not accessible to the public gaze. It is the most secluded spot in Granard town, which is why the young go there when they are mitching from school. It lies just beyond, but enough beyond, the church and the row of houses opposite the church which mark the end of the town proper. Beyond the church and the houses, there is only a hill and beyond that, along the deserted country road, there is only the graveyard.

Unless you turned sharp left up a broad, walled lane and stepped through a gate into a lonely quarried dell enclosed by a tall thicket. High up on the granite face of the dell is the Virgin Mary. She can be seen from the public road, through the evergreen trees. A person lying on the ground at her feet would not be seen. A girl giving birth at her feet would not be seen. A girl might give birth there and leave the baby behind. Other babies, in other places, have been left behind by young girls who then walked away.

A crazy idea in a small town, of course, but if no one knew for sure that she was pregnant, a young girl might persuade herself that she could get away with it.

Is that what happened?

Journalists must ask the family after her death what others would not ask the family during her life.

Don't ask the state or the Church or the people. They did their duty last year, amending the Constitution to ensure that all pregnancies would be brought to full term. Nowhere in that amendment was provision made for life or lives beyond the point of birth.

Those are family matters.

Ann Lovett brought her pregnancy to full term.

On stony ground.

In winter.

Mother and child died.

Why? How?

Ask the family.

Until they speak we'll stand by. You can't interfere with the family, dead or alive.

BISHOP CASEY:
AS SEXUAL AS ANYONE ELSE

IN DUBLIN
JUNE 1984

'**I**'m as sexual as anybody else and there are a thousand ways to express that sexuality.' The person who said that is not Mae West. The words were not uttered by Sappho. Nope, it wasn't Oscar Wilde. Wrong; it wasn't Madonna. The Virgin Mary? You must be joking.

No, no, no, St Joseph never let the words pass his lips.

Listen here now, leave Oliver Flanagan and Charlie Haughey out of the discussion!

Yes, of course, you know a dozen people who've said the very words to you; it's par for the course; promises, promises, promises. We should be so lucky.

Give up?

Wanna try three more guesses?

You'll never guess.

The person who said those words was Bishop Eamon Casey in a *Hot Press* interview. He, you will remember, is the man who sold a hospital on condition that the doctors who bought it from him did not perform sterilizations. He is as sexual as anybody else and knows a thousand ways to express that sexuality.

He isn't a bit shy about it either. He gave a few examples of his personal theological *Kama Sutra*. For married couples he recommends 'shaking hands.' He was quite explicit about it, no humming and hawing and substituting four-letter words as gross euphemisms for coupling. 'Shaking hands,' he came right out with it, is a sexual act.

Bishops, as we know, seldom shake hands. They hold out one bejewelled finger and ask for a kiss on the ring.

Phew!

There are other steps to earthly heaven.

He recommends 'an embrace, putting up with each other, listening, being silent, being tender.'

So far, we've performed seven of the thousand acts he recommends. That leaves nine hundred and ninety-three to go. At which point—orgasm? Ejaculation? Perhaps. Consummation? Certainly not. At that point the bishop withdraws. 'There's a thousand ways in which you express sexuality other than sexual union,' he says. This is odd. The Catholic Church is quite explicit about consummation being an integral feature of the sexual act. Some time ago in England, the Church refused to solemnize the marriage of a paraplegic man and an active woman, on the grounds that the man would be unable to complete the sacramental act. Completion, said the Church, involved the penetration of the vagina by the penis and ejaculation into the vagina. The couple had a thousand ways of their own of giving sexual pleasure, but they admitted they couldn't achieve number one thousand and one.

No consummation, no sexual union, said the Church.

Foreplay, the Church dismissed the couple's bag of tricks.

Nothing wrong with foreplay, of course.

Very good for you.

Shaking hands is not an earth-shattering way to begin, but we have to take account of culture, locality, custom and tradition. The South Sea Islanders start by rubbing noses, after all. Can't see that catching on here. Can't picture Bishop Casey and Barry Desmond rubbing noses, particularly not after the hospital deal. Can't imagine the implications, anyhow. Can't imagine what to think, to tell you the truth, next time I see a picture of some bishops shaking somebody's hand. What, I shall ask myself, do we have here.

Nope.

Bishop Casey hasn't quite got the hang of sexuality. There's a lot more to it than shaking hands, saying nothing, and looking tender. A lot more.

It's rather more vigorous than he imagines.

It hardly bears imagining, to tell the truth.

In fact, it's quite ridiculous, the shapes people throw when they get down to it. There are few positions more ridiculous—to look at—than the positions people adopt when they get together. Limbs everywhere. Orifices gaping. Mucus pouring out and in. Sweat flying. Sheets wrecked. Animals and insects fleeing the scene when the going gets rough. Noise? My dear, the evacuation of Dunkirk in World War Two was an intellectual discussion compared to it. Once in a while, of course, there's silence. Usually afterwards. It's called exhaustion.

You don't get exhausted shaking hands.

I mean to say, tell the truth, when's the last time you saw an exhausted bishop?

Nope, he hasn't quite got it right yet.

FURTIVE LECHERY

IN DUBLIN
SEPTEMBER 1984

I n Lahinch, County Clare, on a recent hot August night, women gathered outside a pub door seeking fresh air. Other revellers, students of the annual Merriman Summer School, remained inside pursuing the hares raised during a week's discussion of 'The Priests and the People'. The theme had seemed particularly apt; the school was founded in 1968 with the intention of commemorating Brian Merriman, whose banned bawdy seventeenth century poem 'The Midnight Court' contained a lusty appeal from frustrated women to priests, urging them to do what the elderly celibate laymen of Ireland would not do.

That particular hare had not been raised during this week. On this one night, however, outside that pub, the women, for no reason at all, spontaneously began to confess to each other. They confessed quietly lest the neighbours should hear. Every single one of them had been interfered with, mentally or physically, by a priest.

Next morning, at a seminar quiet, angry reference was made to the 'furtive lechery' of priests, but the remark was not taken up and no one sought details. That was to be expected. When a few women spoke quietly and publicly some years ago about wife battering, the details were so shocking and the inferences to be drawn about men within marriage so disturbing that the phenomenon was quickly labelled 'Scream quietly or the neighbours will hear.' On

124

this night in Lahinch the women confessed quietly to each other their experiences of priests.

Here are some of the details. Mary, at eleven years of age, was brought during the school retreat into a room to confess to the priest. They were alone. She knelt before him. He pressed her head into his lap. He then asked her if she had ever had sex with animals. He told her never to believe it was right to 'do it' with boys when she was bleeding because she could just as easily get pregnant then. She was eleven and did not know what he was talking about or what he could be feeling with her head pressed into his lap, but as she grew older and learned about life, the memory came back to haunt and disturb her.

Martha, aged fifteen, was confessing during another school retreat and was also alone with the priest in a room. She admitted to French kissing but could not find words to capture the details required. 'Was it like this?' asked the priest, putting his arm around her and his tongue into her mouth. Those are the speakable details. What was remarkable about that group of women, five in all, and comparative strangers to each other, was not the details of their stories but the commonality of their experience. Each one of them had been interfered with physically or mentally by a priest. Some were luckier than others. They were adult women when it happened and more able to cope. The question arises though: how common is the experience to Catholic women? It is a difficult question to pose on many levels. The subject is taboo. Its implications are disturbing. Credibility is hard to establish because one is mainly dealing with little girls. Little girls who complain about fathers are shied away from. Little girls who complain about Holy Fathers would find people steering a wide berth around them. This columnist can complain of nothing more substantial than the priest who picked up her book on Freud, opened it at a chapter headed 'Sex' and admonished

her that it was dirt which should not be read without permission from a bishop. When you're twenty-one, though,
and in search of a teaching job in that priest's diocese and
the job is in his gift, you can be made to feel very dirty
about sex. Your mind can be interfered with in a massive
way if you're in a dependent position. How widespread is
this molestation of girls and women by priests? Confess
quietly or the neighbours will hear, but confess; for it is
widespread, it is damnable, destructive and ought to be
stopped.

THE KERRY BABIES

IRISH PRESS
MARCH 1985

The Catholic Church will break its silence tonight on the Kerry Babies affair, when the parish priest of Kilflynn, who delivers the Sunday sermon at Abbeydorney five miles down the road, will give an interview to the British television programme *TV Eye*.

The investigative TV journalists have spent the last fortnight in Kerry, examining the wider implication of the matter, with particular emphasis on sex education, contraception, and the situation of Irishwomen.

For the first time, the programme will show a headstone recently erected on the grave of the infant found on the shores of Cahirciveen. 'In loving memory of me. The Kerry Baby,' reads the inscription. At the foot of the stone rests a plastic baby enclosed in a clear plastic bubble.

Tawdry though that image may seem, it is radiantly beautiful compared to the harsh realities of Dublin Castle, where the Tribunal of Inquiry hacks its weary and bewildered way though the events of last year, the men sitting under an incongruously placed Bord Fáilte poster of Slea Head, off which one of the babies was allegedly thrown. Last week the public even got an inadvertent glimpse of a post-mortem photograph of the Cahirciveen baby, held aloft by yet another expert on the length of umbilical cords and the weight of newborn infants.

This man, his hands held apart to indicate a certain

127

length, ventured a 'guesstimate' in centimetres which was challenged by Martin Kennedy, counsel for the garda superintendents, whereupon Judge Kevin Lynch produced a steep tape measure, which the expert then used to satisfy their mathematical minds.

A second male expert, speculating on the angle at which umbilical cords might break or be cut, announced candidly, 'I haven't had the opportunity yet to pull a cord off a placenta.' Placentas are precious these days, you see, and are stored in deep freezes the moment they come out of wombs for use in heart surgery and such. The days are long gone when there were 'very well-fed cats in the Rotunda Hospital gardens because they used eat the placentas,' the first expert observed.

The atmosphere in Dublin Castle became quite clubby last week, as first Professor Robert Harrison, professor of obstetrics at Trinity, then Dr Declan Gilsenan of the Midland Health Board took the stand. Professor Harrison even set a little test, inviting the men to work out for themselves the weight of the amniotic fluid in which a baby floated in the womb, given that its volume was '750 to 1000 millilitres at birth.' Judge Lynch whipped his pocket calculator out. His mastery of detail, and ability to convert grammes into ounces, metres into yards, has been favourably noted.

The men had their moments of light relief during classes. After confessing that he found it quite distressing to look at the photographs of the dead Kerry babies, Professor Harrison brightened up when Anthony Kennedy, counsel for the guards, asked him to examine a cutting from the *Daily Mirror* which told the story of a woman who had twins by two different men.

'Which page?' grinned the Professor. Page three pictures of naked women are a famous feature of British tabloids. 'Unfortunately,' guffawed Anthony Kennedy, 'there's no picture with it.'

How the other men giggled!

The men also discussed how a woman might look if she were carrying twins within her. Last January in Tralee, when Judge Lynch asked a female nurse who had worked alongside Joanne Hayes in the Sports Complex if Ms Hayes had looked like she were carrying twins, Anthony Kennedy had objected technically to the idea of giving weight to the opinions of a 'mere nurse'.

Since then much time has been devoted to the opinions of mighty medical men, none of whom had ever see Joanne Hayes pregnant.

Professor Harrison disagreed with Tralee gynaecologist Dr John Creedon's speculation that a woman bearing twins would necessarily have had 'a military bearing'. Some women were the 'mother-earth types who would strut and waddle,' while others 'retain their femininity,' said the professor who has very fixed ideas on what constitutes femininity.

As for paternity, the professor informed the legal men that wives aren't asked too many questions any more in the presence of husbands. 'We are well aware that the father may not be the father and one doesn't want to delve too much into that.'

One English hospital had found that 21 per cent of babies were not conceived by the men who presumed themselves to be the fathers. In the Rotunda, where he regularly delivers babies, Professor Harrison often takes the precaution of not writing down answers given by women expecting twins when making arrangements for possible blood transfusions.

'You can never say somebody is the father. There are things nobody wants to talk about,' he told Martin Kennedy. Mr Kennedy didn't need to be told. The German expert he consulted never published his findings that 2.5 per cent of twins born were conceived of different fathers. 'He said nobody wanted to know,' Mr Kennedy was woeful.

Anthony Kennedy had a message of consolation for deceived men everywhere. The German women who had twins by a German man and a Black American had been unable to claim maintenance from either, 'as paternity could not be proved'.

Judge Lynch cut through the meandering about twins by different men by pointing out that Garda Liam Moloney had been unsuccessful in his attempt to halt the relationship between Joanne Hayes and Jeremiah Locke because she 'was so infatuated or in love that she would not entertain the idea of breaking it off.'

Garda Moloney's initiative had been undertaken in August 1983, 'almost exactly at the time the third pregnancy was conceived.' Which, if the judge is correct in pinpointing conception, means that the Abbeydorney baby was born several weeks prematurely, thus clearing up the mystery of its light weight.

Weight, umbilical cords, fathers, lawyers and medical men aside, the judge proceeded to what he thought was the heart of the matter. 'What sort of ladies are we dealing with here?' he asked Anthony Kennedy about the *Daily Mirror* women. 'We do not know,' he answered himself. 'We do know here,' he referred to Joanne Hayes,

Joanne Hayes says her baby was born in a field, and her aunt Bridie Fuller says the baby was born in the farmhouse. Both underwent psychiatric examination last weekend. The women agree that only one baby was born that night.

The psychiatrist's findings will be presented to the Tribunal, which has now spent eleven weeks pondering the credibility of the garda case that Joanne Hayes had twins by two different fathers, or the same father, one of which she secretly delivered herself in a field, the other of which her family helped deliver, stab and throw into the sea off Slea Head.

'You can never say somebody is the father,' Professor Harrison told the lawyers and guards, all of whom are fathers. Will that affect their deliberations in any way?

What sort of men are we dealing with here?

LITTLE RICHARD

∞ ∞

OUT MAGAZINE
APRIL 1985

The connection between Little Richard and Irish Catholic bishops may at first seem tenuous, even obscure, especially to anyone born since 1960. Not to worry.

All the bishops were born before 1960, and lay people, it may safely be said, did not come down in the last shower as regards matters sexual.

Even the bishops recognize that. People, they have more or less indicated, were born the way they were born, and it can't be helped. Which brings me directly to Little Richard.

Some time in the sixties he took part in a movie called *The Girl Can't Help It*. This movie featured Jayne Mansfield, a woman with a forty-two inch bust. As she strolled across the screen, Little Richard screamed in his inimitable fashion, 'The girl can't help it, she was born to be.' Lest that message escape some folk, Richard repeated the line, so we staggered youthfully from the movies grunting, *The girl can't help it, she was born to be, yeah, the girl can't help it, she was born to be.*

Rock 'n roll, you gave me the best years of my life.

Truly.

Anyway, the bishops, Little Richard, and I are now in tune.

Take the bishops' recent pastoral on love and sex, for

132

example. Remember that Little Richard is now a practising homosexual pastor in the Christian tradition. In other words he ain't no Muslim, nor Hindu, nor pagan. He's a rock and rolling homosexual Christian, sister.

The boy can't help it.

No problem, say the Irish Catholic bishops in their pastoral letter. 'It is not Christian to despise homosexuals and exclude them from society.'

Homosexuals are OK, say the elderly lads.

Furthermore, they say, 'Homosexual tendencies can be innate and irreversible.'

The boy can't help it. Need more be said?

Alas, yes.

The bishop was not born who did not have more to say. These lads can't help it. Pondering that which is irreversible, the bishops engaged in an intellectual *pas de deux* that is familiar to graffiti connoisseurs.

To be or not to be.

Or, as the bishops formally put it, homosexual tendencies 'can cause drives and temptations which are difficult to control or resist.' This being so, 'Some homosexual actions may lack the full freedom and deliberateness necessary to constitute grave sin.'

The boy can't help it!

Neither can the girl!

'This is not a mortaller.'

We were meant to be.

'Each case,' the bishops stressed, 'must be judged individually and compassionately.'

Could anyone ask for more?

Did any reasonable human being, ever, on this earth, ask to be judged other than individually and compassionately? Come back, Little Richard, all is remembered. Christ, you know it's getting easy.

DEATH ON THE BORDER

∞ ∞

MAGILL
MAY 1985

T he young British soldier guarding the border checkpoint between County Leitrim and County Fermanagh stood in the dark under a makeshift signpost. The arrow-shaped boards nailed to a telegraph pole indicated the distance from Manchester, London, Germany, Cyprus and points far, far away.

He did not know, nor did his companions in their concrete fortress know, how to get to Lisnaskea a mere twenty miles ahead. He had never heard of the Graham family, who live down a laneway off the main road in the countryside that surrounds Lisnaskea. Three Graham brothers, all part-time members of the Ulster Defence Regiment (UDR), have been killed by the IRA since 1981. Jimmy Graham, a school bus driver, was shot dead on Friday 1 February 1985 at Derrylin, not far in time or distance from where the British soldiers now proclaimed themselves utterly lost.

'I haven't a clue why men join the UDR,' says the Church of Ireland Rector, Reverend Joshua McCloughlin, who buried Jimmy Graham. The sermon he delivered to the thousands who came to mourn, standing in the open on a wintry day because there was no room in the small hilltop church that normally accommodates less than two hundred, contained a warning. No words of vilification would be unleashed upon the perceived enemy. The rector reserved his scorn, instead, for the civil service, those 'white-collared workers in London and Dublin,' making their plans on 'ever shifting sands' for the future of Ulster.

The rector vaguely disapproves of the whole notion of a locally recruited UDR. 'They're being set up. They're soft targets.' He indicated softly that the gun corrupts, power corrupts, and that neighbours who patrol neighbours run a very slight risk of corruption and a very grave risk of retribution.

In his sermon he had said, 'I'm sure members of the UDR recognize only too well that they are not above the law.' The regiment has come under mounting criticism across the North as a sectarian force, whose members engage in off-duty killing with legally held guns. No such criticism, however, was voiced of the Graham brothers by those Catholics living around Lisnaskea with whom this reporter spoke. They were very much seen as members of the community who were killed just because they were in the UDR. Over and over again the words were repeated 'It wasn't because they were Protestants. If they hadn't been in the UDR they'd be alive today.'

Reverend Joshua McCloughlin points to the irony of that reasoning. It was precisely because they were Protestants, who felt under siege and unwanted, that the Grahams uprooted from Monaghan in the post-Treaty twenties and moved across the border into Fermanagh.

Their small family farm at Corrard near Lisnaskea could not support all the brothers and sisters, and Albert Graham, when his time came, moved out and into a nearby railway cottage to start a family of his own. He reared five sons and two daughters in that little house on a small patch of land at the foothills, working as a labourer and supplementing both his income and social life as a member of the 'B Specials.' His children in turn moved out to marry, working mainly in unskilled poorly paid jobs. Wherever they went, however, they erected the family crest, two eagles, one on each of the gateposts that guarded the pathway to their homes. When the British Army arrived and the B Specials were disbanded and replaced in April 1970 by the Ulster Defence Regiment, Mr Graham joined up along with three of his sons, Jimmy, Ronnie and Cecil, and his daughter Hilary. Fermanagh, which shares the North's longest border with the South, was becoming increasingly militarized. Today the voting population of 63,000 is patrolled by 2318 security personnel, a ratio of one legally armed person to twenty-eight civilian adults, half of whom are disaffected nationalists who once made Belfast hunger striker Bobby Sands their MP. It is recognized by all sides that the IRA incursors are imported from outside Fermanagh.

The Graham family came through the seventies relatively unscathed, though Hilary was hospitalized for several months after being knocked down by a car that crashed through a security checkpoint. She has since died from cancer. The UDR, comprising 260 full-time members and 360 part-timers, lost twelve members in that decade, six of whom were shot dead in 1972, the year of Bloody Sunday,

In 1981, the year of the hunger strikes when the security and Republican profile of the North became more deeply etched, three part-time members of the UDR were killed in Fermanagh. The first to die was Ronnie Graham, a thirty-eight year-old married man with two children. One Friday morning in June he drove his children to school, dropped his wife off at his sister's house and began his lorry round, delivering coal, milk, and groceries to outlying homesteads in the bleakly beautiful moorland that surrounds Lough Erne. He was ambushed at a farmhouse door, on the road to Derrylin, within sight of the Portakabin where his younger brother Norman lived,

At his funeral, which was attended by thousands and where a piper played the lament, the rector said, 'in the normal course of events, his name would not make the headlines ... this family will not be ordinary again.'

Five months later his brother Cecil was shot dead. Cecil Graham had married a local Catholic, Mary Rice, who worked alongside him in the cotton factory at Lisnaskea, and they set up home in another Portakabin. His elderly uncle, a bachelor who inherited the original family farm at Corrard, came to live alongside in another Portacabin, and Cecil worked the holding in his spare time with a herd of sixteen cattle. When the uncle died, leaving him the ancestral farm, Cecil Graham began to build a bungalow on the land, financing the enterprise with the couple's factory earnings and his part-time UDR work.

Mary, who had finally become pregnant after nine years, left the factory when a twelve-hour shift was introduced. 'That left us short of money. Cecil would sell off a beast to buy bricks, finish his shift and go down to build the house, and put in nights and weekends with the UDR.' The current minimum pay is sixteen pounds per eight-hour tour of duty.

They had barely moved into their new home when the baby was born, prematurely and with a heart murmur. With her husband out patrolling at night and the infant ailing, Mary could get little sleep, so she moved back into her parents' home until the health of mother and child was restored.

Her parents lived in Donagh, a village that has been described as the only real ghetto in the county. All forty-nine families there are Catholic. Donagh, in November 1981, was still hung with black flags of mourning for the hunger strikers. On the night of 7 November, Cecil Graham went to visit his wife and five-week-old son. He stayed for an hour, left about 11 pm, and was shot getting into his car.

Mary's father, who had served as a boy soldier with the British Army at Dunkirk in 1945, heard the gunfire, switched off the lights and ordered his family to stay in their bedrooms. He opened the door, peered out into the street and 'saw a hand come up by the wheel of the car. Then Cecil pulled himself backwards up the path, and I brought him into the hall. His mouth and stomach were shot to pieces.' The village remained in darkness.

Cecil Graham died in a Belfast hospital two days later. Despite a hard working life, he had finally finished the bungalow, but left a bank overdraft of five thousand pounds. Mary leased the bungalow and farm, her parents left Donagh, and the two families now live side by side in a council estate in Lisnaskea. Though she married Cecil Graham in the Church of Ireland, and her son was baptized into that faith, she will now raise him as a Catholic, she says. 'Religion doesn't matter, and politics don't matter either, but I'm back with my family and I don't want him to grow up different to his cousins.'

She does not see herself returning to the farm. 'People might point and say look at how I got it.' She maintains contact with the Graham family through one of the two surviving brothers, Kenneth, who is engaged to her sister, 'He met her long before I met Cecil.'

The death of Cecil Graham was overshadowed and overtaken by that of Unionist Assembly member Reverend Robert Bradford, who was assassinated a few days later in Belfast. Even as the loyalist workers of Fermanagh joined in a province-wide work stoppage in protest at the assassination, a married neighbour of the Grahams, Albert Beacom, also a part-time UDR member, was shot dead in the farmyard of his home.

That was also the week when the Reverend Ivan Foster, DUP Assembly member for Fermanagh, announced the formation in the country of a 'Third Force' which would voluntarily and without legal constraint supplement the work of the RUC, UDR and British Army. Masked men paraded through the streets of Enniskillen,

With Albert Graham retired and with two sons and a daughter dead, Jimmy Graham was the only one of the family still in the service of the UDR. A married man with two children, he worked as a school caretaker and bus driver, supplementing his wages with a quite substantial income as a part-time officer of the UDR. His wife Lily had a part-time job in Lisnaskea High School.

The small cottage in which they lived was renovated into a smart two-storey farmhouse with outhouses in which they raised pigs. Jimmy Graham managed to buy four more acres, which he hoped to use for horse breeding. Acknowledged locally as what the minister who buried him called 'a self-willed man,' Jimmy Graham took his military duty as seriously as he took his civilian work.

He had spent three years in the Territorial Army before joining the UDR in 1970, and his service to Queen and country was recognized in January 1985, when he was awarded the British Empire Medal. Long before his brothers were shot dead, Mr Graham had twice escaped ambush, once as he came out of his home, and once when a bullet grazed his shoulder as he drove the school bus.

On the first day of February 1985, as he waited in his bus outside a Catholic primary school in Derrylin, ready to drive children to the swimming pool in Enniskillen, the IRA killed him. He did not have time, the local newspaper reported, to draw the service pistol that off-duty members are allowed to carry at all times. He died a few miles from where his brother Ronnie was killed.

His wife Lily heard the news later that morning as she went shopping in Lisnaskea. She knew that there was something wrong when she went into the drapery store. Everybody was standing there, shocked and staring at her. The Church of Ireland bishop of the diocese flew back from New York for the funeral.

The news of Jimmy's death was too much for Ronnie Graham's widow, Josie. Just two weeks before that a twenty-one year-old part-time member of the UDR had come courting her daughter. As he left the house, a hail of bullets struck him. Although he survived, Josie Graham did not survive the sight of him 'crawling back up the path to the door,' in the words of her daughter. Josie moved her family out of the countryside and into a council house in Maguire-sbridge, and she was brought to a mental home in Omagh, suffering from a nervous breakdown. She is allowed to return home at weekends.

Mary Graham attends a psychiatrist every fortnight.

Lily Graham refuses to speak to reporters from Dublin, saying 'The South harbours the IRA.'

Lily Graham did say to her local newspaper that though she lived in fear, night after night, for Jimmy's life, she had nothing but praise for her Catholic neighbours. They would have come to the wake but for fear of the IRA. One of those Catholic neighbours told *Magill* that he did not dare go to Lily's house for fear of Jimmy's friends. 'And the embarrassment of it. What could I say, when I knew Jimmy would not have been killed but for being in the UDR.' He went to the cemetery and was lost among the thousands who thronged it.

Ken Maginnis, the Westminster Unionist MP for the area and former UDR man and teacher, has called for increased security forces in Fermanagh. A member of the House of Commons Select Committee for Defence, he was one of two MPs who recently volunteered to fly to Norway to observe the British Army and Navy engage in the 'Cold Winter' exercise.

The other volunteer for this thankless courtesy task was a newly by-elected Tory MP. The temperature in the snow-bound wilds of Norway was thirty degrees below zero. 'There is no doubt about Britishness,' said Maginnis on the exercise. 'These are the reasons I was invited.'

Back in Fermanagh, Kenny Graham still lives with his father in the railway cottage, and works with a brother-in-law mending old cars. He refuses to talk to journalists and will not allow his father to be interviewed. He never did join the UDR.

Nor did his only surviving brother Norman. Norman, who works in a Lisnaskea factory, married a local Catholic, with whom he now lives in a Portakabin set on concrete blocks along the small corrugated iron house in which his wife Pam and her eleven brothers and sisters were reared. Pam's bachelor brother is the sole occupant of the little house now, the others having all gone to England. The six children of County Fermanagh's retiring Chief of Police are also living and working in England, incidentally.

Norman, Pam, their infant daughter and Pam's brother, share a small patch of land on which they grow vegetables, raise pet rabbits, and train hunting dogs. Occasionally, duck and pheasant are bagged. The place is bright and neat as a poor and honourable pin. Two eagles on a pillar post guard them.

Away up in the graveyard, the graves of Ronnie and Jimmy lie back to back beneath a tombstone that says 'Murdered by the IRA'. A withered wreath bears the inscription, 'The day thou gavest, Lord, is ended.'

THE MAN WHO FELL TO EARTH

∞ ∞

IN DUBLIN
APRIL 1986

The Pope came out of the sky and descended into Ireland on 29 September 1979. It was a magnificently Messianic moment. The heavens had been cleared for it, and the earth brought to a standstill. All airports were closed, so that no man but John Paul could come down from above. All traffic had been banned in Dublin city so that pilgrims must walk to meet him; all workplaces had been closed all over the country, that the people might be free to greet he who symbolized spiritual freedom.

No other place in the world had made such arrangements, but no other place in the world identified so strongly with the direct inheritor of the mantle of Jesus Christ. 'The Pope is infallible when he defines a doctrine, concerning faith or morals, to be held by the whole Church.' These are the words that echo and re-echo unbidden in the mind, when all other words learned off by heart have faded away. Their meaning is awesome. The Pope knows what God thinks, and says what God means, and the Pope is absolutely right. When the Pope speaks, God is speaking.

The Pope, when we were first taught those words, was a figure unreal as the man in the moon. He lived far away. We would never meet him, nor did we expect to meet him, no more than we ever expected to meet God on this earth.

Then a man landed on the moon.

And going to Rome was as common—more common than going to Killarney, given the cost of a holiday in the West.

But still the aura of magic remained.

Men might go to the moon, and all of us might go to Italy, but the Pope would remain immobile and unmoved, there in the Vatican and deep in the panting heart of Rome. Also, an Irishman would never be Pope. So we kept our distance and he kept his, and the Godliness of it all was right and proper and seemly.

No wonder the nation came to a halt when he came over here. Jesus Mary, and Joseph, I mean to say who would have thought it. I was in Blackrock when his plane appeared in the sky, suspended over Howth. As it came drifting closer, hearts stopped with the wonder of it all. 'There's the Pope,' we shouted, laughing and disbelieving and proud as a chosen people could be.

In the Phoenix Park a million people gathered, happy and carefree and innocent of evil intent as a bunch of babies. Goodwill and good cheer emanated like sunshine, and the sun did indeed shine from a cloudless sky. Ushers and orderlies and security men were redundant. A joyfully corralled nation behaved as if blessed, and thought itself blessed and *was* blessed when he stood atop his Popemobile and was driven up and down and through our serried ranks, so that no one was far from him, and the Irish people felt as close to God as it was possible to be.

He looked the part: handsome, virile, gentle, happy and gorgeously dressed in white silk, satin and glowing gems. We never heard a word he said, but no matter, for the words had been with us since birth, and the ritual of the Mass was an automatic reflex of genuflection.

We went home content, we Irish who had seen the Pope, and next day we switched on the television to watch his progress through Limerick, Galway, Knock, and

Drogheda, and those were the days when the earth turned on its axis and the world as we knew it fell completely apart.

He who was infallible spoke rubbish. Black, he said, was white. Faith fled like snow off a ditch. The Emperor was left with only the clothes he stood in. No one has referred to him since, but his words will never be forgotten. John Paul the Second single-handedly destroyed the authority of the Roman Catholic Church which had held unchallenged domination over the minds and hearts of the Irish nation since Patrick plucked the shamrock.

'Tu es Petrus
Et super hanc petram
Aedificado ecclesiam meam …'

'Thou are Peter, and upon this rock I will build my church and the gates of hell shall not prevail against it. And I will give to you the keys of the kingdom of heaven. Feed my lambs. Feed my sheep.'

*   *   *

This guy blew the sheep off the rock and out of the water.

Woman, he said in Limerick, should return to the kitchen sink. Paid work outside the home was bad for them, for their offspring and for their husbands. Contraception was no good either. This was the equivalent of telling children they shouldn't have pocket money or buy Smarties. Shortly afterwards Dessie O'Malley, Mr Limerick himself, founded a new political party and defined Durex in the Dáil as the apex of democracy.

Murder is murder, John Paul declared confidently in Drogheda, looking north where he had not the nerve to go. 'On bended knee I ask you to stop,' he asked the Provos, and everybody in possession of a telly could see that he was sitting on a chair as he said this, and there was no way, however much the nation still clung to the faint hope that somehow, somewhere he would show himself infallible, that the viewer could be persuaded that a Pope sitting on a chair was also on bended knee.

Shortly afterwards the people of Fermanagh elected Bobby Sands, Officer Commanding of the IRA in Maze Prison, as their Sinn Féin member of parliament at Westminster; Kieran Doherty, also of the IRA, was elected TD for Cavan; and Paddy Agnew, also of the IRA, was elected TD for Louth. Cardinal Ó Fiaich's explanation that people saw their elected Sinn Féin representatives as helpful in matters such as gardening—God help me, I'm on the floor laughing as I write this—was seen as so much ecclesiastical shamrock.

The Pope's visit, said Eoghan Harris at the time, would set Ireland back sociologically ten years for about three weeks. He was wrong. John Paul brought us right smack into the twentieth century, and with only fourteen years to go until we reach the twenty-first, there is every indication that the people will come of secular age right on the button. He untied the Gordian knot of Church and State and personally exposed the fallacy of infallibility, leaving the holy men in frocks in tatters, for which let us give thanks.

God bless the Pope.

CHERNOBYL:
SENTENCE OF DEATH

∞∞∞∞∞∞∞∞∞∞∞∞∞∞∞∞∞∞∞∞∞∞∞∞∞

KERRY'S EYE
MAY 1986

I used to wonder what I really would do when the news came that I had not much longer to live. Generally, I felt that I'd be too sick in bed to give a damn, or too old and frail to book a night out on the town in New York. I wondered if I'd feel bitter about having paid into a pension fund for decades, with only weeks left to spend it. Naturally, I flattered myself that I'd ring up my nearest and dearest, passing on noble wishes that they'd be happy nevertheless without me, and recalling their many acts of love and kindness to me.

It wasn't a bit like that in London last week when the evening papers screamed that 2000 people were dead in Russia, the lethal cloud was on its way to Europe, and anyone living within one hundred miles of a nuclear reactor was living on borrowed time. Standing outside a tube station on the Holloway Road I read the paper and did what everybody else did—got on with normal life.

Try as I might to put my affairs in order over a lovely greasy breakfast, and plan a few really sensational events for the short number of years remaining to me, I could come up with nothing spectacular or noble. I didn't even bother to ring home.

Towards midnight, however—they say it takes a while

for shock to set in—I swung into action. I could have supper in the fish and chipper, or I could dine in a newly opened Indian restaurant where the grilled and spiced prawns were fetching rave reviews. The difference in price between the two places was a small fortune.

Standing at the counter of the fish and chipper, I heard Pete Murray interrupt his late night music and chat radio show to say that the expert on nuclear disaster had arrived in his studio and would be answering questions until 2 am.

I had not heard such somber tones since the Northern Ireland branch of the BBC did an hourly summary on the run-down of the power stations during the Ulster Workers' Strike in 1974. Soon, soon, the commentators said back then, there'd be no more hot water. We were passing the point of no return and the sewers would be flooding the streets and we'd be years waiting for the electricity to get turned on again.

Everybody in Derry believed these guys and my mother kept the immersion switched on all week, and we were all forced to have two baths daily so as not to waste the boiling flow. Months later, when the strike was over and the power stations were working merrily away, the electricity bill came in.

It was enormous.

My mother didn't regret a penny of it.

That week, she said, was the first, last and only time in her life when she didn't give a damn about money, said to hell with poverty, and blow the expense. She would treasure the memory of such luxury for the rest of her life.

So I cancelled my order of ray and chips, turned on my heel in the London café, and went next door to the Indian restaurant. The more the expert lamented the disaster and predicted more—all the waiters were listening to the radio—the more I ordered. I had the advantage of not paying in cash. Using a plastic card, I figured the bill would not arrive for at least a month, by which time wouldn't the world's finances would be in chaos? American Express would surely have vacated their headquarters in nuclear station-dotted Europe and moved to Kerry, and by the time they'd sorted things out we'd all be dying anyway and Justin Kevin Lynch himself would hardly still be holding court, demanding that I account for the errors of my ways.

So I spent and spent for three days in London. The initial shock is now over, of course, and people are reassuring themselves that it couldn't happen here, not in Europe, certainly not in England and definitely not in Sellafield, within whose shadow we in Ireland live.

It also occurs to me that London restaurant owners were on to a good thing, playing the Pete Murray Show loudly over their radios and luring the customers to part with the remaining few quid.

Nevertheless I have not broken off the love affair with my plastic card. News does not necessarily travel fast, and radiation sickness assuredly does not. The fallout from Chernobyl in terms of information and those deadly particles is not yet over by a long chalk. It could be that we are living in very dangerous times.

If we're going to go out with a bang, I intend to go out broke. I'll pay my phone bill of course, and the mortgage and the TV licences and attend to little matters like that. That's called caution.

So now I know: not with a bang but a whimper does a human being meet the end of the world. A couple of prawns, that's all I snatched from it.

A couple of lousy prawns.

EVERY YEAR'S THE SAME

∞ ∞

OUT MAGAZINE
JUNE 1986

There's no point in putting a gloss on it. Christmas ranks as the loneliest day in the year for the person who is gay, unknown to the rest of the family. All over the Western world on 25 December, hearts will beat homeward to the mammy and the daddy. Homage will be paid, extracted, volunteered and involuntarily wrung from the withers.

It is culturally irresistible. It has been bred into us. It has given us some of the happiest moments in our lives, Christmas Day, and the memory lingers on, stirred by the pealing carols, the bright shopfronts, the hint of frost, the smell of turkey and pudding. 'I'm dreaming of ...' we'll hum at the bus stop, and 'Silent night, holy night, all is calm, all is bright!' we'll sing in the pubs and the factories and the offices as the moment draws near, because they're both grand songs and who could stand aside from the impulse towards joy and good cheer that will pervade the meanest group amongst us.

And then will come the day, the one day of the year, when we're all obliged to play at happy families and will seize the chance to do so because the family *was* happy once, when we were children; and who among you would begrudge the pretence that it is still so, would burst the bubble and shout 'Mammy, Daddy, I left my childhood behind years ago.'

So in we will all troop, daughters and sons with our spouses and our children, and those of us with neither spouse nor child, but with a lover left behind in another townland, and those of us with neither spouse nor child nor lover, glad to get in out of the cold. And our mothers and fathers will watch and wonder and wait and pray that not today, not today, Baby Jesus, will the family front be breached.

They know, of course they know, that for the other 364 days of the year their children are not what they seem to be. Parents did not come down in the last shower; the relationship has not been thought or wrought that is unknown to them. But that does not mean that words have to be put on these things. They may never have put words on these things but they know; it's just that one day a year they prefer not to know, as we prefer not to remember that once there were shouts in this house, and tears, and cruel words.

That's life.

The 25th is not a day for life; it's a day for impossible dreams. It is a day for the most impossible dream of it all—that Jesus, Mary and Joseph were a normal unit. Impregnated by a ghost, what? Pregnant outside marriage in the eyes of her community, what? Gave birth in a stable among the animals, what? Never slept with her elderly husband, not once, what?

Put like that, and taken in the context of her time two thousand years ago, when women were stoned to death for adultery, when nobody believed in ghosts, and the unmarried mother of any Kerry baby would never have survived as far as the courts, there is some comfort for the gay person. Mary had it rough too. A lesser woman lying on straw would have told the Three Wise Men bearing baubles to fuck away off.

She didn't and we won't. Not on Christmas Day. We'll stay away or we'll keep quiet. There are 364 other days in which to win friends and enemies to a redefined notion of family; on this one day the mammy and the daddy would like a rest. Jaysus, they're entitled to it, sure they never meant us any harm, and they only wished the best for us.

Goodnight Jesus, goodnight Mary, goodnight Joseph. Happy Christmas, sisters and brothers. Who're ye tellin'?

THE LIFE AND DEATH
OF MARY NORRIS

IRISH PRESS
JULY 1986

Four weeks before her life ended, Mary Norris told me that she would welcome death. The month after that interview, those who knew her—neighbours, welcome officers and community workers alike—sensed that another disaster was approaching. They did not anticipate death, or the deaths of her four daughters.

Now that it has happened, they acknowledge bleakly that the circumstances of Mary's life were such that death must have seemed a release to her. She fell all the way through the welfare net. Try though they might, and many tried to help her, nobody knew how.

Mary moved like quicksilver on shifting sand. At the core of this wise-cracking, resourceful, childlike, childish and illiterate young woman was loneliness. 'The only good thing to come out of me disasters is that the neighbours come round. I like that. I like the company,' she told me.

She was sitting at her kitchen table at the time, talking about yet another fire in her house. While she spoke, the women were making tea, bringing in clothes collected in the area to replace the burned ones, sweeping up debris, washing down the sooty walls. All the electricity in the house had been switched off as a safety precaution, save that in the kitchen which Corporation workmen left functioning. Her husband Jamesy was up in Finche's Pub.

Mary hoped the *Irish Press* would publicize her story and help her secure a bigger, brand-new house around the corner. The damage to her living room did not justify such a move. A coat of paint and fresh wallpaper and rewiring would have left the house as habitable, though as empty as before. The furnishings were meagre. The torn wallpaper in the bedroom and hallway had been like that before the fire of 10 June 1986 which caused the neighbours to contact this newspaper.

Another new house, another new start, would only have provided another setting for the disasters that regularly engulfed Mary's life. House fires had already occurred in her previous Corporation homes in Blanchardstown and Ballyfermot. They were all small and all relatively non-threatening—the family had always survived.

Each time they moved, they moved on to another welfare file and another police file, bringing their innocuous catalogue of inadequacy along with them—an unemployed husband who drinks. A wife who took small overdoses of Valium, children who attended special schools, a barring order against Jamesy, a small succession of dodgy welfare claims, a weekly appeal for Supplementary Welfare from the local Health Centre—just another poor family in a country where one third of the population is living on the poverty line.

Mary used some of the resources advertised by the Church and devised many of her own. Her life was a catalogue of hard work, its sole end the procurement of the one thing that she could understand very well, money. Much of that went to Jamesy, the rest on rent, fuel and food for the children. For herself, she demanded only cigarettes. The things that money could not buy, such as parenting skills, affection, literacy and financial management, were beyond her reach.

A community worker recalls talking with Mary about food. She suggested that instead of tinned steak and kidney pie and bottles of lemonade, Mary should shop for other things. The community workers offered to accompany Mary to the supermarket. Mary agreed, then took to her bed saying she couldn't face it. The worker spent Mary's money for her, bringing back a bag of potatoes, mince, eggs, and vegetables.

'Look, Mary, that'll keep you for a week.' Two days later Mary landed round in the welfare office to cadge some supplementary benefit. 'The kids don't like that kind of food. I have to buy the old stuff,' she said. The nuns enrolled Mary into their housekeeping classes. One of her closest friends remembers Mary's attendance at the kitchen school.

'She loved being among the women. She kept us all in stitches with her jokes and her stories. She disrupted us entirely, and then she dropped out. She said she preferred to eat the tinned foods.'

But Mary grew on people. A Free Legal Aid lawyer whom she visited in the Law Library every fortnight remembers the first time her met her in 1973. 'Her marriage had only started. It was in trouble. She was tiny and thin, and had a quirky humour. I took to her.'

Some time later, the lawyer came across Mary begging at the entrance to the Hibernian Hotel. He resumed the relationship. 'She'd come down to the Law Library once a fortnight, and I'd give her a cheque or cash. She'd tell her stories, I'd half listen. She'd receive her money, which was really all she came in for.'

Neighbours do not know the name of another benefactor who saw to it that Mary's ESB bills were paid. Mary's excellent status with the ESB ensured that she was able to buy a ghetto blaster on credit shortly before the fire in June.

Speaking amid the ashes of the June fire, Mary pointed to the transistor and said she had bought it for her daughter Catherine to help the girl forget the fire that had engulfed Mary's mother's house. Catherine had been staying with her granny in Ballyfermot when a blaze killed the granny and Catherine's uncle.

Mary's mother was of travelling people stock, but she married and settled down with a local man. Her friends remember Mary at fifteen, selling paper roses in Ballyfermot. By sixteen she was pregnant, then married. She stayed close to her parents, going to her mother several times a week.

After her mother burned to death on 15 April, Mary was plunged into grief. An intimate conversational outlet had been destroyed. 'She loved to talk. She came down her every Monday looking for money, but you knew perfectly well that she really wanted a conversation. She was lonely,' says a member of the Rowland Health Centre.

She always brought some of her children with her. Sometimes she left them behind in the Health Centre, saying she wanted them taken into care. But then she frequently adopted a similar attitude to Jamesy. One day she wanted rid of him, the next she wanted to stay with him. After a few hours in the Health Centre, the social worker would bring the children back to Mary's house a few steps away. Mary would ask if the children had been given their dinner and if they had, she would grin with delight. She had seen to it that her children were fed, one way or another, another small victory to chalk up against the failure of her mothering skills, which the cot death of her baby Shirley years ago seemed to represent to her.

She took her own steps against Jamesy, obtaining a court order barring him from the house on grounds of assault. He wandered on back home anyway. Sometimes, when it got too much, she telephoned the guards from a neighbour's house. She informed them anonymously that it would be worth their while to check the Norris home for stolen goods. They might lift Jamesy and take him away for a while, she explained to her neighbour.

Mary had arranged years ago that social welfare payments be made out separately for her and Jamesy. He got 36 pounds a week for himself, she got 74 pounds and 35 pence for herself and the six children. Because she was illiterate, the neighbours filled out the necessary forms for her, every year, declaring the circumstances.

Mary's hard work included petty shoplifting. The Judges always let her go after hearing her stories. The last conviction, she told me, was for stealing a pair of black slacks which she needed to wear to her mother's funeral. Under gentled nudging of her memory by a neighbour, Mary realized that she had stolen the trousers before her mother's death.

That she needed clothes, there is no doubt. Her money always went on the others, particularly to Jamesy. Sometimes, when the women decided to go to Finche's for a celebration of their own, Mary would wear Catherine's confirmation outfit. She was so thin and small the child's clothes fitted her perfectly.

She was so thin that the Health Centre allowed a special payment of ten pounds a week for a dietary supplement for her alone. It was not felt, however, that she would spend the money on herself. An arrangement was made with a supermarket that the cheque supplied to Jamesy would be spent only on good food for Mary.

Jamesy had been used to making his own arrangements for what he considered were his and Mary's needs in Finche's Pub. He asked that she not be allowed in before ten o'clock after the children were safely in bed, and then only if he were in the pub himself. In that last week of Mary's life, Jamesy's request was made redundant.

Mary was barred by management from going in there without him around, because in the days before her death she had taken to going round the pub collecting money to replace the furniture damaged in the June fire. She concentrated on customers whom she deluded herself did not know her. Mary was tirelessly and anonymously organizing a benefit collection for her own family. It was foolish but it was funny and neighbours cheered her ingenuity.

She didn't often go to Finche's, but when she did she amused her friends by her antics in getting round Jamesy's pub decree. She would drop to her hands and knees and secure a table out of his sight.

Living on the edges of society, Mary had a gift for cheering other women up. As one of her friends put it, 'I will never forget what she did for me. One night in the pub the lights went out and a barman appeared with a cake lit with candles and Mary started singing "Happy Birthday". She had arranged the whole thing. For the first time in my life other people knew it was the anniversary of the day I was born.'

None of the women for whom she arranged these treats minded at all when Mary called around next day and borrowed money to keep her going. She was scrupulously careful to repay her debts to her neighbours in feast and famine. She often lent them money herself.

Her children sensed that begging and repaying was a way of communication. The night of the final fire, Fiona and Deirdre had gone up and down the road borrowing tea bags. A neighbour decided to call in and see if Mary was in a food crisis. There were plenty of tea bags and need of none. The children's allowance money had been paid out only that day and Jamesy had given her some of it.

Mary and the neighbour burst out laughing and went on to celebrate Mary's latest stroke of luck. Thanks to donations from the Gay Byrne Hour and a welfare supplement, a kitchen suite was installed in the repaired living room, and only that night a second suite had been delivered to Mary's door.

The neighbour did not question its provenance because Mary had so many stories to explain things. Instead, she sat on this second suite in the kitchen, marvelling at it. She knew it might or might not be sold outside the back door, as Mary was often wont to do when a deluge of luck came her way. Where before there had only been a humble table and chair, the new suite added to the kitchen fire and smoke that later killed Mary and her daughters while they slept.

Mary's mother had worried about her daughters. When she discovered Catherine bleeding before the age of ten, she consulted the other women about early menstruation. The women spoke to Catherine, and Catherine talked about a man in a van who had offered her lollipops and touched her. But there had been no menstruation. The neighbours advised Mary to take Catherine to hospital. Mary later said that one hospital had talked of sexual interference while another dismissed the notion, and the guards are checking out the stories now.

A community worker to whom Mary sent Catherine for sex education wonders in retrospect if Mary was sending yet another signal for help. So many stories from Mary, who did the very best she could, scrabbling for money for her family while living an outwardly laughing life of the deepest loneliness and despair. She married young, she died young, and she never had the leisure or opportunity to grow up. Since becoming a child bride, she was preoccupied with being a mother.

It's hard enough being a mother if you know how to be, and have a partner who knows how to be a father, and both have the time and maturity and freedom from financial woe to acquire the skills. Love is not always sufficient, although among the very poorest love is all they have to offer.

A voluntary worker, who discussed the plight of the Norris family after Mary had spoken with me, offered a consolation born out of experience in an area deluged with deprivation. 'Children can survive anything,' she said.

The four Norris girls did not. For Catherine, twelve, Sabrina, eight, Fiona, seven, and Deirdre, three, there was no more salvation than there was for Mary, their mother.

DIVORCE: SPLIT HAPPENS

HOT PRESS
MAY 1995

Brace yourself, Brigid.

One more referendum, to allow divorce, and we're out of the jungle. Peace North and South, civil liberties for all, nothing more to do but consider what kind of country, what kind of people we want to be. It's really all over, the great social debates, political quarrels and gunfire of the past twenty-five years. Contraception, abortion, divorce, gay rights, the war with Britain. The fire has burned out, the smoke is drifting away, and we begin to see clearly now. When the next millennium comes—a mere five years away—the landscape for the young will have vastly changed.

What we have just gone through will be ancient history to them, just as World War Two is ancient history to us. In the going down of the sun and in the morning, future wee gits should remember us, and thank us. They won't of course. They will look with pity upon us as we recall times past and secretly think us barbaric. How could we have tolerated such antisocial legislation as that which was written, amended, and re-written into the Constitution, they will ask among themselves, as we talk among ourselves about the way we were?

Then they will have their cake and eat it, the ungrateful wee bastards, without so much as a word of gratitude for us who baked it for them.

Do I care? I don't care. I'm not one for the glory days. No sad sack me, in the corner of the café with the old soldiers, while Springsteen sings a lament for our inability to live in the present. I'm scarcely concerned with the present, come to that. It's the future I'm looking to.

The present is still littered with obstacles. Forces stir in the undergrowth by the side of the road, hoping to entangle us again. The British government will drag its feet; Pro-Life honchos will fight to the last gasp; there are endless details to be tidied up. It will be a while before abortion, already legal, is available.

Divorce will be available, but it will be a while before anyone can obtain one—they want us to spend five years in marital limbo, the way they used to make unbaptized dead babies wait between heaven and earth. It will be a battle all the way to freedom. We can handle it. The war itself is over; these are the mere remaining skirmishes.

It will be tiring, yes; irritating and debilitating, yes, as we fight the last of the rearguard actions. An awful waste of the present yes, but the future is ours. I can wait. I've got plenty of time. The future is ours, I tell myself every day now, as we gallop headlong towards it. What will Ireland be like in the new millennium? The truth is, I don't have a clue. I only know it won't be like the past, and I never want to see the past again. The odd thing is, I can hardly remember the past.

For instance, I cannot remember what exact kind of uniform British soldiers wore in the streets of the North, though they only came off the streets of Derry a month ago. You'd think, wouldn't you, that if you saw one of those guys in your bedroom, pointing a gun at you, that you'd remember every detail for the rest of your life. In my day (what a way to talk of British soldiers!) I have seen thousands of them—in my bedroom, in the attic, in the street, every time you'd open the door, they'd be there, and yet I

161

cannot say whether their tunics buttoned to the throat, or if they wore shirts underneath.

As for the Pro-Life arguments and the counter-arguments we put up against them, don't talk to me about them because every word is gone out of my head—though there was a time in the eighties when I was a walking, talking expert on the inside of a woman's womb, and the even more complicated insides of the Pope's brain. How theologically sophisticated feminists quickly became who hadn't been inside a church since they discovered the theory of the multiple orgasm.

Now you'd have difficulty finding a priest to chat with, never mind argue with. Clonliffe Seminary took in only twelve students this year. The male priesthood is a vanishing species. We shall not see their like again. You wouldn't want to, if you'd been through the last twenty-five years. And there's no guarantee that women will rush to fill the vacuum when a Pope comes begging them to consider ordination.

No more than women or men will rush to enter marriage. A five-year wait for divorce? Soon, very soon now, there will be a five-year wait before heterosexual couples, snug in the one bed, will even consider marriage. And their parents will be the first to urge them to make haste slowly. I take it for granted that people in a gay relationship will show the way and treat love as a purely private matter, using the law only to secure property details.

Where it will all end? Sure, I don't know. In peace, privacy and honour between individuals. Far from ending, this is only the beginning. We don't know where the road will lead us. We don't know what we are capable of, even. For the first time ever in Ireland, we are out of the trenches, standing on our own two feet, asking each other what is to be done next?

What a great question that is. What next? Forward to

the future, sisters and brothers. See you there. I'll be the one with a smile on my face, breathing deeply of air that is fresh, tasting social freedom.

Just one more referendum. Brace yourself, Brigid. We're winning.

SARAJEVO SIEGE

∞ ∞

SUNDAY TRIBUNE
AUGUST 1995

I am disabled by apathy. To my bed by 9 pm, conserving candles for the long dark days that descend next month. The nights are noisy—mortar and machine gunfire, the rasp and whine of UN tank treads, dogs howling at every shot. Who keeps that cock that crows just before the Muezzin joins in?

The woman of the house rose at 6 am and then set off for school at 7 am to prepare for the coming school term. Though children are taught at home, their parents bring their homework to school, for correction by the teacher. With her departure, all the energy is sucked out of the apartment. Her husband and child stay sleeping in the bed in the corridor—four-walled protection against mortar—until 10 am. Sleepless, I stand on the balcony and watch her run through the smoke rising from the rubbish that burns in the metal wheelie-bins—modern waste disposal, Sarajevo, 1995.

The dump outside of the town is dangerously within mortar range. The woman turns and waves to me, holding her nose wryly against the smell. Full of energy, or spirit, she sweeps the third-floor stairs and foyer all the way to the bottom every day. I watch an off-duty soldier and two boys pluck handfuls of clover from the grass verge beneath the apartment block and stuff it into sacks. Food for animals or for themselves?

Ho-hum, yawn, stretch; it is now 8 am. I look to my

left, to the ruined outdoor skating rink, where the Winter Olympics were staged in 1984. I look at the hospital opposite, where Radovan Karadzic used to practise psychiatry.

At 9 am I slip past the sleeping father and child, wrapped in each other's arms, and go into the dark bathroom. Gradually, I adjust my sight to the gloom. I sit in the empty bath placing a half-full bucket of cold water before me, and pour the first plastic cupful over my head. If this is bad, what will winter be like? I console myself, and later my hosts to their delight, with the thought that though there is piped water in the fabled a-hundred-pounds-a-night Holiday Inn, it is never hot.

I pray that I can pee while I wash, thus avoiding the waste of precious water down the toilet. On rainy nights, unknown to my hosts, I pee onto the tiled balcony in the dark.

I think the family upstairs has gone as daft as myself. They fiddle until 3 am every night with a short-wave radio, tuning in all over the world. They cannot possibly understand all those languages.

A clever family farther along has refashioned part of a tent from the holidays of yesteryear into a canvas canopy over their balcony garden. It is a few inches short of the garden's length and depth. When the canopy is bellyful of rainwater, they tip it onto the crops below.

The Red Cross told me that initially they spent as much time counselling city people on how to adapt to a calamitous fall in living standards as they did teaching them how to live by third-world methods, growing food from seed and pickling and preserving it for the winter. Instruct the residents of Dublin Four to dig up their rose-bushes and plant spuds and there you have it. Switch off their fridges, TVs and videos, take away their cars, put them on welfare, tell them this might go on for years, and you get the picture.

Nonetheless, my food is served up on china, and we use good silverware. My landlady's parents, who have a private house and huge garden, supply their relatives with fuel; but they are down to their last tree. I hope to Allah it is a big one.

Sunday is the official day of rest in Sarajevo. I could not find a mosque, church or synagogue open. In the afternoon, I reverted to the habit of my childhood, when we used to spend the doleful Protestant Sabbath walking around Derry's beautiful cemetery.

The prewar headstones and tombs in Sarajevo are a delight, an art gallery of East European, Moorish, Christian and Jewish stone-masonry. Plain, small wooden crosses mark the descent into suffering and cruelty since 1991. Each cross bears the year of death and the victim's number in the roll-call of death for that year.

Victim number 908, in the year of 1995, was Addzic Esma. And a hundred yards away, I happened on Victim number 909, 1995, Palosevic Ismet. I saw three freshly dug empty grave plots. Must be ready for all eventualities, mustn't we?

There are many cemeteries in the city, usually deserted because they are a favourite of Serb gunners. If number 909 was the most recent victim, that makes one hundred and thirty dead per month from a population of 300,000 as of Sunday, 30 July 1995, though some, of course, die from natural causes.

The number wounded monthly is higher. Taxi drivers try for a tip by showing you shrapnel and bullet scars. My landlady showed me drawings done by some of her pupils. A ladybird, a man chopping wood in the park, a still-life of blood-spattered corpses and limbs lying in the street.

The level of mental illness in Sarajevo is quite high, ranging from depression to severe disturbance. Certainly, the husband in my apartment lives quietly on his nerves. He spends an inordinate time on the phone or stretched on the sofa or fiddling with the radio, seeking news. I have never heard him laugh. A gentle fellow, it is clearly an effort for him to return my silly smiles.

I saw the first really insane person last Sunday afternoon. He ran down the middle of the street, bare-chested in the rain, wearing shorts and Bosnian Army boots and socks. From his mouth protruded a whole lemon; he rang a silver bell with his right hand. he held a bunch of roses aloft with his left.

Emulating the Statue of Liberty? The Olympic torchbearer of 1984? Some people smiled, some turned away, unable to bear the sight. Nobody stopped him as he openly courted sniper fire.

It occurred to me as I sauntered or ran along the mainly deserted pavements that a mortar landing half a block away could shake loose the jagged shards of glass remaining in the windows high above and that my head might be sliced off. Maybe the fellow wasn't so mad after all?

I took to the middle of the street, zigzagging. Girls embracing their soldiers at barracks gates stared at me. I returned to the pavement. Psychologically, Radovan Karadzic isn't such a bad strategist at all.

One truly wonderful thing happened to me last Sunday evening. Though all the restaurants which depend on electricity were closed, I stumbled upon a shish-kebab café where cooking is done on a charcoal grill just behind my apartment block. Bosnian soldiers on leave were inside drinking cheap local beer. One of them was a magnificent singer. He belted out the great ballads of his country, wailing, beguiling, arousing by turns.

For one blissful hour all my troubles melted away. I might have been in a pub at the Merriman Summer School, listening to David Hanley and John A. Murphy serenade each other with the great Irish ballads.

Then curfew came, and we dispersed. Sunday evening coming down, dropping deadly slow, the baleful crump of mortars the only music of the night.

Last Monday night the lights went on all over our sector in Sarajevo after an electricity supply was secured via cable through the tunnel under the airport.

With luck, our sector would receive four hours every Monday night, and return to the use of candles from Tuesday through Sunday while other sectors got their once-a-week share. My landlady vacuumed, I did the ironing. We shampooed our hair in hot water and watched TV all evening.

It was bliss to be a housewife.

VERONICA GUERIN

HOT PRESS
JULY 1996

The man from the BBC interviewed me about the riot and I observed it wasn't much to write home about. Not compared to what's going on in Dublin, he sympathized. What was going on in Dublin, I asked, having been with English football fans all day? He hesitated. Veronica Guerin had been murdered, he said.

He told me this at two in the morning in Trafalgar Square, in London town. I walked away, wandering down a side street, looking at the cars which had been smashed. Then I wandered back, listening more closely now to the language used by young and not so young men, drunk out of their skulls. Cunts, fuckers, bastards.

One of them bumped into me, grinned in a friendly way and called me missus. I was glad, for the first time ever, that my hair does indeed seem to be grey to the onlooker, though in my fond mind it seems more goldy, streaked with silver. The young man obviously considered me to be no danger. Veronica's hair was fair. I only met her once, at a meeting we both addressed. I was struck by how unassuming she was. Many journalists have egos as big as houses.

Sometimes, reading an article they've written, you realize that the conversation you had with them the night before matches word for word the article you've just read. The conversation had been rehearsed, polished, honed from hours of fine print, not spontaneous at all. In the couple of hours I spent with Veronica Guerin, she never mentioned the work she did. That was so unusual, it made an impression on me.

Now she's dead, dead, dead. Many other journalists have been killed in the course of their work, but for most, the bullet that ended their lives was random, impersonal, a shot fired in war that could equally have killed the person standing next to them. Few have been killed because of what they write. The day after Trafalgar Square I sat at a pavement table outside a café and was shocked by an English tabloid article about football. The writer was bemoaning a German striker called Kuntz. 'He would be called that, wouldn't he?' wrote the man from the *Daily Mirror*. It's the first time I've seen a journalist refer to someone as a cunt. I've often heard them do so, but write it? Never.

One of the drug barons who threatened Veronica Guerin called her a 'cunt'. Effing cunt. Cunt this, cunt that. There was much use of this word in Trafalgar Square. Then in the tabloid paper. Then in the mouth and mind of the man who threatened Veronica. Cunt, as you know, is the popular generic term for the female sexual organs. Used properly, it can be beautiful. Cunt is lovely if you like sexual congress with a woman. The man who uses it as a term of abuse is abusive about women. The worst thing he can say about another man is that he is like a woman. Cunt is the worst thing he can say. Many men don't realize that. They are surprised when I point out that they are degrading, rejecting, mocking that which they otherwise claim to love. Sure they've only used the word casually, they point out. It points up a casual attitude to women, I rejoin.

I have to say here that I once used the word as a term of abuse. Just once in my whole life. I was looking for a word that would express my total, utter revulsion about the

men who had tried to kill me, who had killed thirteen
others. I said it in the kitchen of my parent's house in Derry,
hours after Bloody Sunday, when we were talking about the
British soldiers who had carried out the massacre. 'Cunts,'
I said. At any other time, my parents would have been
revolted. Maybe they were that day, or in too great a state
of shock to notice, or maybe they wisely chose silence in
face of the clear shock that I had undergone. They never
mentioned it ever afterwards. I never apologized. Maybe
they knew how ashamed I was that I had taken the name of
women in vain in that way, but still, I can't get way from it
—the worst thing I could intimate about the soldiers that
day was that they were objects to be despised, that they
were 'cunts'. When a woman can be brought to despise her
own sex, you know how devalued life can be for all
women—we are objects of ridicule. That puts us in danger.
We become an endangered species. Cunts, flies, gnats—
swat them.

This is not why Veronica Guerin was killed, though her
womanhood contained the seeds of its own danger. The rise
of woman journalists in the past decade has been noted.
Commenting on this, Mary Holland reflected that women
were getting the scoops, throwing the journalistic media
punches, because they didn't know the rules that had been
keeping men hidebound in hitherto all-male clubs. Sean
Duignan ruefully noted the powerful presence of 'The Sisterhood' when he was government press secretary. Male
political correspondents could be massaged because they
owed favours, because of the male bonding that went on
between politicians and the fourth estate, because, well—
men sympathized with each other in tight corners. Then
along came the outsiders, the women who had no understanding of how the game is played.

If Veronica Guerin knew the rules, she broke them. I
have no idea whether she did or not, but she was different.

She spoke to the men who deal in drugs. Had conversations with them. Engaged them in chat. Had one of them in her own home. How very womanly. Whether they took extra pleasure in the fact that she was a woman when they had her killed, I have no idea either.

And I am painfully aware that Jim Campbell of the *Sunday World* received no such massive outpouring of solidarity when he was shot by loyalists who objected to his exposure of their deeds. One difference is that Jim didn't die. He had to leave home, now lives away from home, but he didn't die. Also, he is male, and I think that makes a difference in public attitude. This implies that men are somehow expendable; that it is expected that men will be killed in this man's killing world.

For some time now in Ireland, men and women alike have been killed, as a matter of casual form, in gangland wars, marital disputes, fights outside the chip-shop, fatal rapes. It has taken the murder of Veronica Guerin to make the government shout stop. The baddies killed a citizen, set themselves up as a State within a State, declaring their absolute right to kill citizens who opposed them. This was indeed a watershed, and its reverberations might yet spread to make us take account of what we have casually tolerated in our own government-run State, the killing of citizens by citizens.

The devaluation of life begins in the word, in the mind, in the attitude. When I think of the murder of the journalist Veronica Guerin, I shall forever think simultaneously of the male journalist who formalized in print, with the sanction of his editor and no outcry from his union, the debasement of human beings, of women, of 'cunts'.

JUKEBOX

∞ ∞

HOT PRESS
AUGUST 1997

Saturday afternoon. Pocket money. Best white blouse with a fitted string bow-tie. Convent grammar-school blazer to show I was not a corner girl. Thirteen years old. Alone. Solitary. Not at all embarrassed to hang over the jukebox by myself. Women and men in couples, drinking coffee and eating ice-cream in wooden booths with leather seats. Glorious smells of vanilla and roasting beans, a cool breeze wafting through, an open sun-lit doorway. The occasional sound of a bus trundling past and a sense of great pedestrian bustle in the street outside. Not much traffic in Derry 1957, but enough to annoy me. The grinding roar of gears changing might wipe out the precious plonk of a guitar string. Elvis did not have a big-band sound then. A passing bus could bury the occasion.

Such a sacred occasion. One record for threepence, five for a shilling, which was twelve old pence. If I chose one, the Italian owner of the café might feel entitled to move me on. I was blocking the narrow passageway. If I chose five, the money would be gone in a short splurge and I'd be back out on the street, a whole other week to before hearing the beloved again, up close and personal. Listening to the radio was not the same at all. The sound came thin over the airwaves from a pirate station out on the ocean, and I was hardly ever allowed stay up late enough to hear.

Sometimes I chose one record and then bought a

wafer, also priced threepence, and loitered over the jukebox, making the ice-cream last, hoping an old person with money to burn would include an Elvis record when making a jukebox selection. Sometimes I'd go for broke, spending the entire shilling on five Presley recordings. That would be an anxious time, guarding the jukebox, warning prospective clients that I'd already chosen 'Heartbreak Hotel,' steering them towards lesser-known works. That's how I came to appreciate 'Blue Moon'. If I was lucky, someone would play 'Hound Dog'—again—after I'd played it. Saturdays like that, you'd die of bliss. Hormone-driven bliss in a miasmic cloud of romance. *Blue moon, you knew just what I was there for, someone I really could care for ....*

The someone wasn't Elvis as such. I'd seen a photograph of him in a movie magazine which my aunt brought home from the cinema where she worked. He had flipped down the strap holding a woman's dress up over her shoulder and was autographing her bare upper arm. There was a sulphurous look on his face. I knew I wouldn't be able for that level of sex. My aunt nearly died when she saw me studying the scene. She snatched the magazine from me. His voice coming from the jukebox was as close as I wanted to get. I used to bend forward to see his name inscribed on the record label. Elvis Presley, it said. Wondrous to behold. Magic. Elvis Presley and me. Which is why I went to the café alone. You wouldn't want another person present at a time like that.

The next year I allowed another girl accompany me on my mission. My parents by then were allowing me to go up the town on Sunday afternoons and evenings. The reason I brought the other girl along was that there was another Italian cafe on the other side of the bridge, well beyond the inner-city limits my parents understood me to patrol. The other café was over in the Waterside, a Protestant redoubt, and it was favoured by American sailors stationed on that side of the river. They smoked cigarettes and it was rumoured (and faithfully believed) that they played cards in the café late at night and had sex with women. Kissed them on the mouth right there in the café, after midnight. The café had a jukebox and more Elvis records than any other.

Hence the girl I brought along as my companion. She had nerve. Confidence. An aura of knowing. She wasn't afraid to kiss anybody. Not that anybody asked, for we were young and idiotic compared to the older women in lipstick and stuff. This girl brought me to this café one Sunday evening at 9 pm and we had chips and lemonade, bold as you like, and we stared and stared and she wasn't frightened at all. The café-owner's daughter was boarding at our school, which we figured was some kind of protection. The American sailors played Fats Domino and Jerry Lee and Little Richard, penance if you were waiting on Elvis but not the worst penance. At least we got to hear the sailors sing along, in authentic accents, flashing glorious white teeth, their beautiful tanned skin glowing in a way you normally only saw in technicolour movies. And I, sheltering behind my rampantly heterosexual companion, got to hear Elvis.

Oh, Elvis. The day he died, twenty years ago this month, I tore a photograph of him, in all his glorious pouting young manhood, out of the *Evening Herald* and clutched it to my bosom and went round the Dublin pubs and got drunk and went home to a beloved who scolded me for not ringing to say I'd be late. Some people just don't understand.

FAREWELL TO ROBBO

HOT PRESS
SEPTEMBER 1997

So farewell, my President. This is one from the heart. People will talk, rightly, about how you brought the marginalized in from the outskirts. But not nearly enough emphasis is placed on the fact that through you a huge number of us—the 'well-heeled and articulate,' to quote a man who once expressed distaste for intelligent women with aspirations and jobs—identified for the first time with the State, and with all our hearts. Which is why I have amused myself this past seven years with calling you 'my President'.

This is not to say that I viewed the post-Robinson State uncritically. Far from it. It is to say, rather, that for the first time ever I viewed myself as part of it and with a voice that would be fully heard; that I wanted to play a full part in affairs of State, and that the enthusiasm with which I joined in was unexpectedly pleasurable. Before you took office, my President, the State was an entity I fought against, regarded with distaste, and never even remotely considered membership of. Before you, it has to be said, the State wasn't much interested in the likes of me either. Apart from anything else, in the eyes of the State I was just a woman. Taking everything else into consideration, the State and I were poles apart.

That sense of alienation applied to most of the population, I think. Those of us who did not belong to political parties, the vast majority, lived almost totally private lives—with occasional if increasingly frequent forays into the public arena to block the passage of whatever sacred cow they'd just invented, or resurrected, or kept artificially alive. It was great fun being an outlaw, mind you, throwing stones and words, and at times it was far too easy—like shooting fish in a barrel, so moribund, palsied and bereft of imagination was the opposition—but it was not a truly constructive way to live. Entire generations have stood outside the system, with all the waste that entailed. Our brains, hearts, souls and sinews went unused, in the service of the State at any rate. There was no way in, and no way that we wanted to get in.

With you came the concept of citizenship. When you stepped in, the rest of us flooded through the breach. That's actually too aggressive a way to put it, as though we and you have been at war with the rest of the State. It was more subtle, and awe-inspiring than that, now we look back.

Once upon a time, we did not see ourselves as citizens. But literally overnight we issued ourselves citizenship papers. We made ourselves part of the State. This is no exaggeration or impossible flight of fancy.

I remember vividly the morning you took the oath and took the office. It felt so natural. That was the morning I found myself smiling and murmuring 'my President'. The phrase was delightful, the concept pleasing and yes, all right, I took a bit of pleasure in saying it over the next while when I found myself in the company of the former opposition and yourself, at whatever occasion. And yes, alright, there was a bit of divilment in saluting your *aide de camp*, me that had never had much reason to identify with a uniformed officer of the State, but in fairness there weren't many female army officers in evidence before you came along. Certainly none that were publicly entrusted with protecting the likes of a president or even a taoiseach.

177

Now it has got to the stage, my President, that I sometimes forget I'm a citizen. How quickly we take that for granted, a mere seven years to consider citizenship a normal part of what we are. An obligation even, that imposes on us the duty to ask not what the country can do for us, but what we can for the country. All of that because of you. Not because of what you did, because you did not do it alone. You know better than anyone how the people of this country worked alongside you because you've put in the miles. However, you brought unique qualities to bear, and I do believe we should salute greatness where we find it. It could not have been done without you. It could only have been done with you.

And now you're going. Mná na hÉireann will come from all over Ireland to stand outside the GPO this Saturday, 6 September 1997 to salute your departure. You have let it be known that you want the occasion to be specifically open to men, and it will be—though I'm reluctant. For a start, I didn't see them get up off their behinds to organize a tribute but that's men for you, they expect women to do the work. Typical of you, my President, to upset the applecart even as you go, asking for even more than we thought necessary.

For you, I'll do it, but they needn't think this citizen is going to take your departure lying down. See? You're not even gone yet and already the old hackles are rising. Seven years of a feminist presidency was not nearly enough. It was, though, wonderful.

THE RACE FOR ÁRAS

HOT PRESS
OCTOBER 1997

Áras an Uterus? Mad cow disease? Let us now mourn the absence of men from the race for the Park. David Norris would have made a great candidate, and three fellows in the Oireachtas did propose him, but the other fellows in that mainly male institution declined to back him. There's men for you now. Interestingly, several men who were approached by Fianna Fáil and Fine Gael and given first choice ahead of the women who eventually won nomination, declined the offer of the job.

Leaving aside John Hume, who considered himself so far above the dogfight of Free State party politics that he would only accept unanimous assumption into heaven. What sin did Albert Reynolds commit by refusing the immaculate conception of President Hume? The refusal of the other men bears scrutiny.

Former Fianna Fáil minister Ray MacSharry is now a wealthy businessman. Former European Commissioner Peter Sutherland appointed by Fine Gael, is now a wealthy businessman. Neither man would touch the Park with a barge pole, though both could easy easily afford the drop in income from hundreds of thousands annually to a mere one hundred grand a year.

Men on huge salaries have taken a drop before for the honour of serving the country. Lawyers, for instance. Dermot Gleeson cleaned up during the Beef Tribunal, there was a queue to hire his expensive services again for other tribunals, but he turned his back on all that to accept the post of state Attorney General at a comparatively paltry wage. Could it be that some men couldn't face the huge political fight which a race for the Presidency now entails? It used to be that all a fellow had to do was spout party policy, rely on party faithful to get out the party vote, and sleepwalk to the Park.

Then along came Mary Robinson. Seven years later, the contest has become one in which candidates have to put forward ideas, engage in intellectual debate, and articulate 'the vision thing' that defeated the cerebrally challenged George Bush Senior. You only have to listen to the men of Fianna Fáil trying to enunciate Professor Mary McAleese's policy to realize just how difficult it is. The poor hapless fellows can't even read her lips. All them big words.

The nurturing, embracing stuff has so many men and some women running away that the awful question arises: what are they like in bed? One is reminded of the long running farce across the water, 'No Sex Please, We're British.' These people should get a life. French kissing is but one step away from the kiss on both cheeks which the presidential campaigners are showing a happily alarming tendency to adopt. Mary Banotti's European experience might yet go to all our heads and by the way, don't you just dig her call for legalized homosexual marriage?

Not that this columnist approves of marriage under any circumstances, but anything that adds to the gaiety of this nation has to be welcomed, what? And don't you just dig the rock and roll U2 addition to Adi Roche's bandwagon? Street cred, or what? It's far from where we were reared on Dev's comely maidens dancing at the crossroads.

The real reason most men haven't run for the Park is a contradictory one. They feel it's too much work being President and not real work at that. Men see their role in steering the ship of state as one of a captain lashed to the storm-tossed mainmast, cutlass between his teeth, pistol in either hand to shoot the opposition and a pair of steel-capped boots to kick dissidents between the legs.

They believe real men wielding real power don't waste time receiving boy scouts and old age pensioners and community activists worried about a garbage dump on the doorstep and women in the Áras. There are so many women knocking on the Áras door moaning that the menopause is political, childcare should be professionally paid, and mothers want to work outside the home, that a President can't get out any more to play golf.

Gone are the days when in it was a job for a boy, and a good ol' boy taking it easy at that. But there's women for ye now. They'd work at anything. All she needs is the air that she breathes, Adi Roche sings. What in nuclear hell is she talking about? What's fresh air got to do with anything?

FREE WINNIE

∞∞∞∞∞∞∞∞∞∞∞∞∞∞∞∞∞∞∞∞∞∞∞∞∞

SUNDAY TRIBUNE
NOVEMBER 1997

Winnie Mandela put her arms around Archbishop Desmond Tutu and gave him a bold kiss on the mouth. The couple laughed, hugged and kissed again for photographers. Winnie can cheerfully kiss any man she likes now. Former heads of the security branch secret police testified on Friday that they had lied during the apartheid era when they said she was having an affair with Tutu, who still lives near her in Soweto outside Johannesburg. They lied about her after Nelson Mandela was released. She was 'not a nymphomaniac,' nor was her daughter Zinzi; she did not use marijuana, she was not an alcoholic; she had not had an affair with Chris Ball, the head of Barclay's Bank, which was positively disposed to dealing with the ANC.

A full-time dirty-tricks 'disinformation' unit Strategic Communication (Stratcom) had been set up specially to target Winnie because if they could discredit her, they could discredit the entire ANC, the unit head Mr P.F. Erasmus told the Truth and Reconciliation Commission, TRC. They concentrated 'more on Winnie than on any other person in the entire ANC.' This was partly because the leadership was in exile, in jail or on the run. It was also because, says a TRC member privately, Winnie Mandela was, and is, a potent, beautiful, glamourous, defiant, sexy woman living alone in a deeply sexist society. 'The ANC men never gave her a formal position of leadership. She was cast in amber as Nelson's wife, mama, the mother of the nation. They resented her for not being a compliant silent wife, like Walter Sisulu's wife.' The ANC Women's League, also relegated to support roles, adore her as a symbol of women's struggle—though they concede she managed to have a good time while she was at it.

The homely technical school where the hearings are taking place are plastered with posters exhorting 'real men' to use contraception and take responsibility for their partners and children. The posters are for domestic consumption and contrast vividly with the internationally sulphurous whiff of sexuality that surrounds Winnie Mandela. The 'disinformation propaganda,' said Mr Erasmus had 'spectacular success,' using 'forged documents' and untruths, with such worldwide anti-communists and conservatives as John Major and Mr Andrew Hunter. Hitherto classified documents supplied by Mr Erasmus to the Commission claimed smears successfully planted with *Vanity Fair*, Jean Rook of the British *Independent*, *The Sunday Times*, *The Times* and the *Daily Express*.

Since he retired in 1983, Mr Erasmus ended his testimony, he had been falsely accused himself of having an affair with Winnie. The accusation, he later told the *Sunday Tribune*, had emanated from former members of Ms Mandela's vigilante group who are now in jail, and seeking amnesty for crimes committed while they were members of her infamous Mandela United Football Club, MUFC. One of those members, Jerry Richardson, the middle-aged football coach, was convicted of the murder of fourteen year-old Stompie Seipei. Though Winnie's house was surveyed, and her phone bugged twenty-four hours a day at the time, Mr Erasmus told the Commission that 'at no stage did I ever receive information to the effect that Mrs Mandela had killed Stompie or for that matter ordered anyone's death'.

He used informers from within the Club. He apologized formally to Winnie at the end of his testimony and they shook hands. He is now retired on sick pay.

While Mr Erasmus testified, Jerry Richardson, surrounded by amiable prison warders, took notes. Mr Richardson attends the Commission daily, awaiting his turn to testify. His lawyer vigorously rejects suggestions that his client was a paid informer. Jerry insists that he was acting on Winnie's instructions. He hopes his evidence will secure him an amnesty. He and Winnie don't speak. Jerry, smelling of pomade, missing most of his teeth, his trousers rolled up to his knees, is conspicuously dull of mien and demeanour and the hundreds attending the Commission treat him with disdain.

Winnie also didn't speak with Stompie's mother Joyce, who sat humbly one row behind her all last week. 'She has never spoken to me,' says Joyce, speaking to the *Sunday Tribune* through an interpreter. Joyce is one of the few people here who cannot speak English at all, a sign of poor schooling in a country where elementary education is prized above all. A large, shambling, modest woman, she has had two children since Stompie died. 'He would have been my support in life,' she says. She would 'forgive Winnie if she asked me, though I will never forget my son. Winnie is too pompous.' Even Winnie agrees that Stompie met his death in the compound of her house, though she denies being there during the days of his dying.

A succession of the poor and humble of Soweto, relatives of those who died or disappeared during the reign of the Football Club, last week testified to going to Winnie's home, seeking information. Lolo Sono's father begged her to tell where his son, a member of the Club and an alleged informer, lies buried. Mr Sono sheltered and helped the young guerillas of the ANC and worked with Winnie. Then came the dreadful years of 1986-1990, when the ANC resorted to outright warfare and a State of Emergency was declared. After 1986, 'she wasn't the Winnie I know, she was very aggressive, she was completely changed in her face. You could see anger in her face.' The police would not search her house though he asked them to when his son disappeared in 1990. Nelson Mandela was released that year.

'She was almost feared by the State,' Mr Erasmus explained the police refusal to touch her. 'Any move against her would have upset the applecart. There was a general feeling she should be left alone since she was digging her own grave anyway.' Former ANC publicity officer Murphy Morobe echoed his analysis. Mr Morobe had often visited Winnie when he was a student. He discussed 'the cult of the individual' with Nelson Mandela when they served time together on Robben Island. 'Before you mess with a powerful person you must be clear on the facts.' The facts of her involvement with the Football Club were never clear. 'Anyway, the fear around Mrs Mandela was not her problem. It was that of the people and the State.'

The former Mandela family lawyer Azhar Cacalia, who is now head of the Secretariat for Safety and Security, agreed. A month after Stompie died, in 1989, he was a member of the ANC Crisis Committee which called on Winnie to disband the Club. Nelson Mandela backed the call. She refused. 'We decided to publicly distance ourselves from Mrs Mandela's actions. It was one of the most difficult and proudest moments I can remember.' After her husband's release Winnie 'settled old scores,' warning him to stay away from Nelson.

Winnie did not hug Morobe or Cacalia. The aged, crippled Walter Sisulu, lending moral authority to the hearings by his presence, conspicuously ignored her. His wife, who will testify that the doctor for whom she worked disappeared after refusing to sign a 'natural causes' death cert for Stompie, exuded cold anger. The doctor's elderly parents, members of the Indian community, who want Winnie to say where their son is buried, cannot catch Winnie's eye or ear.

She will testify next week. The Commission hearings were suspended yesterday to allow her to open the Mandela Family Museum in Soweto. The museum is the home that she shared with Nelson after marriage and during the thirty years of his imprisonment. It was set alight during the Emergency by students who objected to the vigilante activities of the Club. She moved out then and into a newly built, relatively plush but claustrophobic fortress compound nearby, complete with separate housing for her security guards. The Women's League and international admirers paid it for.

President Mandela would not be attending the opening of the museum, said Winnie's embarrassed secretary. He might, said the ANC, come from Cape Town to attend the reburial in Soweto today of three 'martyrs' whose remains were recently exhumed from unmarked police graves. 'Their blood has nourished the tree of liberation,' say the posters advertising the ceremony. Winnie did not receive an invitation to attend, her secretary confirmed. She wasn't sure what her father would be doing this weekend, said the flamboyant Zinzi, who has been attending the hearings with the Mandela's other daughter, the quiet, older Zenani. 'The only thing you can be sure of after this week is that my mother is not a nymphomaniac,' says a smiling Zinzi.

'She was always friendly, even when we interrogated her in the prison cell,' says a puzzled John Louis Mc-Pherson, former head of Stratcom, now head of administrative police services in Johannesburg. He once planted a successful media lie that the IRA had been invited to the ANC annual conference. He officially recommended Paul Erasmus for 'outstanding performance' against Winnie. 'The club members beat Stompie too much that night,' he says. 'Blacks just don't know when to stop. They weren't professional. I don't believe she was there. The best we ever had on Winnie was her necklace liberation speech, when she praised the burning of informers by placing a tyre filled with petrol around their necks. It reminded us of the IRA's ballot box and araldite.'

MO MOWLAM

∞ ∞

HOT PRESS
MAY 1998

Great images those, of Mo Mowlam in action. Bald and barefoot, striding the corridors of Castle Buildings, twisting elbows the night they worked till dawn on the Good Friday Agreement.

The head of information in the Northern Ireland Office, NIO, Andy Woods, who has just retired early, did not like Mo—though he insists this has nothing to do with the fact that she had him shifted.

Nothing to do with Drumcree last year when Mo, then a novice, was persuaded by the NIO that Orangemen should walk Garvaghy Road. Andy just didn't like the way Mo swore, effing and blinding, and he was taken aback at the way she'd put her stockinged feet on the desk, taken off her baseball cap and gone bald-headed, so to speak, at the British problem in the North.

He was particularly sniffy about her habit of sending RUC minders out to buy Tampax. Such behaviour was a far cry from the manly demands of such former secretaries of state as Reggie—'What a bloody awful place. Quick, bring me a double Scotch'—Maudling.

Mo didn't even sing—it was Andy who arranged for Peter Brooke to render 'Clementine' on *The Late Late Show*, the night seven Protestant working men were massacred. Andy tipped Gaybo off that Brooke had a fine 'basso profundo'.

Though Andy is no more, Mo hasn't gone away. It should not be beyond her wit to facilitate the efforts of the Northern Women's Coalition to remain centre stage in the forthcoming Assembly elections. Monica McWilliams is receiving belated recognition as a skilful operator, and the media increasingly turn to her for a candid, fluent analysis of the situation there. The challenge to convention, and the risks taken by the Coalition, were recently highlighted by the revelation that Pearl Sagar, from the loyalist working-class East Belfast, was forced to move home.

She is married to a former British soldier and her daughter is engaged to a Catholic. These women have served as lightning conductors for the male chauvinism and ingrained sectarianism of the North, and their presence in the Assembly would help dredge up and drain off the poison in the system that will remain for some considerable time.

On 22 May, before the elections in late June, there is the referendum on Articles Two and Three and a simultaneous vote on the peace deal North of the border. It would be easy to punch logical holes in both propositions, which purport to fit square pegs into round holes. And yet it will be done beautifully. The deal is akin to that which a Pope will one day have to sign on contraception and women priests. Both are impossible, says the Catholic Church, and both as sure as night follows day will be introduced by the same Bible-thumping men come the millennium.

How they will word the volte face is beyond me, but how words were found for the peace agreement is equally beyond me. It means two opposing things, both valid. The peace deal guarantees that the North will remain British and guarantees an open door to a United Ireland. The unionists have the moral assurance, underpinned by internationally binding legislation and changes in Articles Two and Three, that they will never be coerced into unity as long as they can muster a majority against it, and the nationalists have the practical means, through North-South councils, underpinned by internationally binding legislation, to bring about unity by persuasion and consent.

If one leg of the deal collapses, the whole lot collapses and everybody gets their money back. I am reminded of the slogan that was swiftly painted on the wall of a bookies shop in Derry, weeks after the war began in 1968: 'We want better odds.' I think this deal delivers that.

As for the guns—trust and rust is your only man. Ask Proinsias de Rossa, much admired by Unionists who worked with him when he was a government minister. Before it became Democratic Left, Proinsias's party had an armed wing, the Official IRA, which didn't hand over one revolver after declaring a ceasefire after shooting John Taylor, now deputy leader of Trimble's party, bombing the British Army base in Aldershot, killing waitresses, mounting a machine gun in the Bogside and inviting us to try it out. Children, women and men queued around the block for that exercise in ballot box and armalite tactics. Proinnsias knows better than most how the transition to parliamentary politics can be smoothly organized.

He and John Taylor, singing from the same hymn sheet, could provide backing for Elton John at the post-Assembly party in the grounds of Stormont by showing new Ministers such as Gerry Adams and Martin McGuinness how the impossible becomes possible. Proinsias and John would be an example to us all.

That I have lived to see this day! And they said it couldn't be done. What next? A free Viagra pill for every man who signs up? A lot of these guys are over forty now and feeling the strain.

NOTHING TO DO WITH US

∞ ∞ ∞ ∞ ∞ ∞ ∞ ∞ ∞ ∞ ∞ ∞ ∞ ∞ ∞ ∞ ∞ ∞ ∞ ∞

SUNDAY TRIBUNE
JULY 1998

One night, Sky television showed a policeman lay his baton on the head of an Orange youth. Once, twice, three times, four times. I did not pity this boy. Had he been a nationalist, I would have, but twenty thousand Orangemen were battering the barricade at Drumcree and there was pure fear on Garvaghy Road about what would happen should they break through. I relished the Sky replays of the scene. I was flintily aware that the North has coarsened my heart. When news came through later that a young woman had been blinded in the eye by a plastic bullet, this heart sank.

We have seldom seen on television—because it is horrible—the amateur footage of Emma McCabe, the Catholic mother who staggered blindly through a Belfast street in 1971, her two eyes torn out by a plastic bullet. The Protestant woman is twenty-one year old Pauline McCullough. What took this university student to Drumcree? She wasn't even born when the Troubles began.

Nothing to do with us, we nationalists might say, North and South. Just as it had nothing to do with us that after the Quinn children were buried in a Catholic church at Rasharkin, a Protestant church was burned in Hillsborough. Very well then—what about the other Northern Protestant churches that have been torched since the stand-off began two weeks ago, and the Orange halls that have been burnt, and the bombs intercepted at Armagh and Newry, and the discovery of petrol bombs in the Republic on the night of the Twelfth, allegedly in the possession of four men allegedly waiting for the Donegal Orangemen to return home?

Nobody died during anti-Drumcree protests by nationalists, we will point out. Now where have we heard such words before? Ah yes, out of the mouth of Ronnie Flanagan, chief constable of the RUC, after the Quinn children perished, when he called on the Orangemen to decamp. 'That was protest, this was murder.' The protest resulted in one hundred and forty Catholic families being burned out of their homes. An acceptable level of protest, so to speak.

On both sides? There has been no discernible rending of garments by nationalists about the fallout from their stance. Not this time—this columnist hopes the Orangemen will be snagging turnips in Drumcree all winter long. That will teach them. History will have taught young Pauline McCullough many bitter lessons. She was a child when ten Protestant working men were shot at Teebane, when Protestant parishioners were shot as they prayed in the church at Darkley, and eleven Protestants were blown up at the War Memorial in Enniskillen. Nothing to with us? Our churches were not forbidden to IRA funerals. This columnist thought the IRA campaign legitimate.

Her history began long, long before she was born. William Butler Yeats had people like her in mind when he said of the Protestants on this island 'No petty people we'. Not just her—my great uncle Ned was a Belfast Orangeman, who strolled through the Bogside in his sash before and after Partition, to pay a visit to his sister, my granny, who had converted to Catholicism to marry my grandfather, the policeman. He stood in the scullery while Catholics recited the rosary at her wake and attended her funeral Mass. He returned for the funeral Mass of her husband, the RIC/RUC sergeant. Was my uncle, with his one arm and one leg left behind at the Somme, really a fascist, as some would characterize the Orangeman? Yeats was ignored and Protestant beliefs were ignored when a law prohibiting divorce was introduced to mark the ethos of the new State. Even as Protestants began leaving for the North we rammed the lesson home by inserting into the 1937 Constitution a clause proclaiming the special relationship between the Catholic Church and the Republic. Our Protestant President Douglas Hyde must have had a lonely time of it after that. He had to lie alone, anyway, in his coffin in the Protestant Cathedral in Dublin while the Taoiseach and the Cabinet stood outside, paying respect at barge-pole length, upholding the tenets of a Catholic religion which said that participation in a Protestant service was a mortal sin.

God, but we were slow learners. 'I am an Irishman second, a Catholic first,' declared the future leader of the 'sixties will be socialist' Labour party, Brendan Corish. He agreed with his Church's hierarchy that mothers and children should not be given free milk. Six years before Pauline Mc Cullough was born, we finally excised the special relationship clause and began going into Protestant churches— unlike the Orange Order which still heinously prohibits its members, under oath, from participating in papish services.

'Sure we get around that rule easy,' says the chatty caretaker of Dan Winter's cottage, where the first-ever meeting of the Orange Order was held. They worked out, she smiled, that going inside a Catholic church wasn't the same as actually partaking in a service. This past two weeks that same caretaker has been tending her sick Catholic neighbour whose home-help has gone on pilgrimage to Lourdes. Last Tuesday, Orangemen who were relatives of the Quinn boys carried their coffins into the Catholic church, stayed for the service and carried them out again.

Pauline McCullough was recovering from the loss of her eye in hospital during that sorrowful day.

While Pauline grew up—and the eighties were only yesterday, in the adult scheme of things—the South went through convulsions over contraception and abortion. It was only three years ago when she was eighteen that we reluctantly legalized divorce while simultaneously opposing the trailing of Orange coats through Catholic areas. While Paisley and Trimble danced their foul jig we were—and still are—coping with the disintegration of traditional Catholic culture. Bishop Casey had fathered a son, the stone had been rolled back to reveal widespread clerical paedophilia, a government fell, pillars of Church and society came toppling down. How did this look to a young girl, making her way to Drumcree, to defend what she saw as the last stand on Protestant culture? Orange halls had already been set to the torch, have been during all the years of her growing up.

Her elders should perhaps have known better—just like ours? Who are her elders anyway? David Jones, spokesman for Drumcree, a minor civil servant and a man younger than myself, grew up in a flat in Carleton Orange Hall in Portadown, where his father had a part-time job as caretaker in addition to his day job as coalman. Recalling the Twelfth of his childhood, Mr Jones remembers his mother spending the day roasting sides of beef in the oven and his father cleaning the toilets in preparation for the hungry brethren returning from the field. Humble tasks by a humble family in service of a cause he calls noble. Orange culture, noble? Sure, look at them, prancing around in their sashes. Not at all like our lads, with their stewarding sashes and epaulettes at Knock.

An unfair comparison. Knock is not at all comparable with Drumcree. Pilgrims to Knock do not put their feet on Protestant ground no more than nationalists in the North stamp on Protestant turf. If anything, we ignore them, another way of stamping on them perhaps. Our history shows that we have ignored them for as long as the Republic has existed. We haven't a clue who Pauline McCullough is, or why she went to Drumcree. Does she know us? Would our history withstand her scrutiny? Her poor, blinded scrutiny?

RESERVOIR PRODS

∞ ∞

JULY 1998

'Take off your mask and put away your gun,' they shouted at him. He burst out laughing and agreed to abide by the law. They clapped and smiled as he mimicked the removal of a mask, turned his back to them, inserted his plastic card, and drew out money. 'Drinks on me,' he announced at the beginning of the annual July Twelfth holiday fortnight. It was a miserable enough start for the small, quiet crowd in front of City Hall, Belfast, that had marched from Shankill and Sandy Row.

The empty streets and shuttered shops made a ghastly mock of celebration. The people of no property marched behind elderly men in modest suits whose orange sashes were the sole source of brightness on a dull Friday evening. What has the Orange Order done to Belfast, less than two weeks after the Assembly met there to seal the peace deal? A group of Italian tourists, sealed behind the locked doors of their deserted city centre hotel, peered out gloomily. They were confined to quarters for the night. It was only nine o'clock.

They'd only be there half an hour, a woman said, adding 'I hope' as she looked up at the rain-clouds. She quelled the children perched alongside her on a window ledge. A man in a blue collarette opined that the Drumcree crisis would not bring down the Assembly no matter how it turned out. 'That's not what we're after. Some yahoos have

196

been causing trouble, we just want to march.'

Pearl Sagar, co-chair of the Women's Coalition, is sympathetic to the yearnings of Orangemen. A Protestant from East Belfast, her soft approach contrasts with that of Monica McWilliams, the Catholic co-chair, who says that 'the howling game' at Drumcree 'does need to be stood down and this is the year that has to happen.' Ms Sagar agrees, firmly, that the law must be upheld and that the decisions of the Parades Commission should be respected in Drumcree, 'and the Ormeau as well,' but she empathises with the sense of cultural loss felt by the community within which she was reared, which she loves. 'I'm a unionist with a small u.' She wants dialogue and believes both sides are intransigent, citing the barracking of Seamus Mallon on the Garvaghy Road 'by his own people'. Nationalists are not sensitive to the fact that the Orange Order was born in Portadown two hundred years ago, she argues.

The people of East Belfast have spent the past week trapped in their own homes by people from their own area, she says in a voice tinged with anger and rue. 'It's mostly young people on the barricades, and not all that dangerous, but we can't afford to go downtown and risk having our cars hijacked and burned when we turn a corner. This community is poor enough.' All bus services end at 7 pm. The teatime news bulletins end with detailed traffic reports on which streets in which towns have been closed by protesters. The reports are upgraded through the miserable night.

Belfast feels more cautious than sinister. 'Any trouble up your way?' was the question, cheerful rather than fearful, passengers posed to each other as they mounted and dismounted from buses going through East Belfast, heartland of Unionism. There are conspicuously few of the Orange Order posters that feature a mother and besashed father holding hands with their two children under the slogan 'Accommodation, not segregation.' There is red, white and blue bunting on every street across every thoroughfare, though, holding out the promise of a great party. Like the run up to Christmas, it's in the air and in the mind. You don't even have to go to the bonfire to experience the spine-tingling pleasure of the occasion. The Twelfth is the apex of the Unionist calendar.

'I had warm pineapple last night. It was delicious,' said a woman to the passenger beside her on the bus journey to loyalist Braniel. 'My Chinese was closed,' came the response. 'Absolutely delicious,' the woman reminisced. 'I hope mine is open on the Twelfth,' said the other passenger. The two women gazed out at bored campers under a tent pitched on a traffic island on the Newtownards Road. The banner above the tent asked motorists to honk their horns if they supported Drumcree. A placard declared that Mo Mowlam was a 'culture vulture'. The women giggled. Some campers at Drumcree have taken to describing them-selves as 'Reservoir Prods'. The people on Garvaghy Road wonder if they are now to be regarded as 'Reservoir Dogs'.

Braniel is a bleak estate, high and hilly and windy and Godforsaken. The bus parks briefly at a green space among the flag-hung houses. The grass is piled high with wooden palettes, old tyres, branches cut from the trees that weep on the overhanging mountain. The young saplings, planted on the edge of the green to cheer the place up remain untouched. Teenage boys shift the palettes aimlessly. If it were after six, says the driver, the bus would probably join the stock-pile. He is not an Orangeman but he wants the parade to go through Drumcree. His tone is wistful. If only Brendan Mac Cionnaith were not in charge of Garvaghy Road. Who then?

'We'd have to check the substitute,' he grins cheekily. He says it would be better to negotiate passage than have the Orangemen break through the army cordon. There would probably be deaths if that happened and if the Garvaghy residents went out to stop them, 'the way they tried to stop the police last year. When people are angry, and the Orangemen would be angry ....' He is sincere when he hopes there will be negotiations and glad no Catholics had died so far. The marches are the last thing they have left, he says. The majority Unionist population will be outnumbered after the Republic 'sends forty thousand families up here to live and swell the vote'. Why would so many people make such a sacrifice when Orangeman are already complaining about going down the road to spend a week in a field? Conversation splutters to a halt at this silly exchange.

Statistics aren't so silly in relation to Drumcree. A majority of Unionist Assembly members, thirty-two out of fifty-eight, are members of the Orange Order, a ratio of almost two to one. An estimated one in ten adult members of the Unionist population are Orangemen. Assuming supportive wives, sisters and girlfriends this figure rises to four out of ten, plus a massive number of sympathizers. Drumcree has become more than a local dispute.

'We feel penned in, as though everywhere we turn there are nationalists cutting what ground remains to us from under our feet, having one parade banned after another and now we're tearing ourselves apart in the cul de sac,' reflects a university graduate who is not an Orangeman. 'If we could just get out of Drumcree, get down that road, breathe a little, we'd have more trust in nationalists.' He welcomed the dialogue, even at one remove, between the Garvaghy Residents Coalition and the Orange Order. 'If we could get just a few Orange feet on that road on Monday, a dozen men bearing standards, we could kick the Order later for putting us in this position. They played the Orange Card and Blair rejected it. Whatever happens, the Orange Order's power is broken.' He mocked the Order's strategist David McNarry for expressing a wish to return to 'the carnival days' when an Orangeman would return after

199

the march to his village, roll up his trouser leg, and put his jacket on backwards. 'That went out on BBC 2. That's what he reduced us to. That's what McNarry will be left with when the dust settles.'

In the early hours of Saturday morning a young Catholic couple checked into the hotel where the Italians were staying. Having received threats to their Belfast home in a predominantly Protestant street, they were taking this step 'just to be sure'. Later, a neighbour rang the hotel to announce the doleful news that a petrol bomb had been thrown into their house. The police were rung in turn and an RUC escort arrived at the hotel to bring the husband back to secure what might be left of their home.

LIGHT MY FIRE

∞ ∞

HOT PRESS
JANUARY 1999

I f you like smoking cigarettes, go to Spain. Let the Germans and the Yanks ruin everywhere else in Europe with their politically correct flared nostrils. In Spain, the hotel receptionist lights a cigarette before relieving you of your passport. Bizet wrote an opera based on Spain's tobacco trade. Did you know that?

Carmen was set in the Tobacco Factory in Seville. It is still there. It looks like a palace, was meant to look like a palace, and is now a faculty of law. It was built in homage to the central part played by the tobacco industry in Spanish commerce. The entrance portal features the carved head of the America-Indian who introduced the new arrivals to the delights of the scented weed. He is a big, noble, contented looking fellow, complete with feathered headdress and pipe sticking out of his mouth. All around him are stone galleons, sails unfurled, running home before the wind, bringing home the precious booty.

Once through the great wooden doors, a series of marble halls lead into enchanted courtyards where fountains used to play while the women took a break from making tobacco fortunes for the boss class. So precious was the weed that the women were strip-searched before they went home after a long day's work. Carmen was one.

The tobacco industry later spread to the satanic mills of Belfast and Dublin, with which there is no comparison.

Suffice to say the boss class here had even less respect for the workers, which perhaps explains the absence of an Irish version of tobacco dance. Try humming 'Woodbine' instead of 'Toreador' and you get the picture.

Hum 'Toreador' and you begin to grasp the esteem in which tobacco is held in Spain, particularly in Seville. As you approach the former factory and light up in anticipation, the thrill runs from head to heels. It's as good as that first cigarette was in rainy downtown Derry. Better in fact, since passing Spaniards murmur 'olé,' recognizing a kindred spirit. The bullring is across the river, just as it was in Carmen's time. Old photographs show the toreadors marching out of their hotels in full regalia, cigarettes dangling gloriously from their fingers. One guy is shown with a cigarette between his lips as he is carried wounded from the ring.

Most carriages on trains are for cigarette smokers, which is why you need to book early. Losers are compensated with cushioned seats and generous ashtrays in the corridor between compartments. Attendants pushing trolleys sell cigarettes by the carton and they are cheaper than duty-free.

Most art galleries allow smoking in the corridors. This is extremely civilized since trailing around galleries can take hours and a person needs to take a breather. In the hairdressing salon it seemed positively churlish to refuse the ashtray proferred while one's hair was being washed, even if it was difficult to smoke with one's head bent backward over the basin. By the time you get into a cathedral it seems strange to see signs forbidding tobacco. But that's alright—smoking is allowed if you make the effort to climb all the way up to the belfry. Have you ever sung 'Carmen' from the top of the Cathedral in Seville? While smoking? It's really quite difficult. Not impossible but difficult, given the climb. Even the gargoyles are coughing.

Spain has to be the last place in Europe where a haughty gentleman pauses to light the senora's cigarette before sweeping her into the restaurant. Certainly it's the only place where the motorcyclist paused to light a cigarette before revving up and relieving my companion of her shoulder-bag. The police were sympathetic. 'Your tobacco was in the handbag?' There are ashtrays on every desk in the station.

ABOVE THE LAW

∞ ∞

HOT PRESS
MARCH 1999

If you are an Influential Business Person or IBP as the banks put it, they write off your debt rather than incur the wrath of your rich VBF's—your Very Best Friends. Allied Irish Bank has told us so, explaining why it cancelled Charlie Haughey's overdraft. AIB was afraid that some of CH's VBFs would switch their business to another bank, in protest, and CH's VBFs had a lot more money than CH and used to give our poor, mendicant Taoiseach the change out of their back pockets.

AIB was right and all. Better to sacrifice a million than lose a billion in the long term. AIB knew perfectly well what it was doing; it set a sprat to catch a whale. Taoiseach Charlie had the confidence of the business community and it was just a matter of time till the sprat brought the whale on board. Charlie was good for the country, the country was good for business, business was good for the bank. AIB is now the richest bank in Ireland.

I was a sprat myself once, so I know. I used to write a column for *The Irish Times* called 'In the Eyes of the Law'. It was all about how some buck-ignorant District Justices in the lower courts at the Bridewell maltreated petty criminals and social derelicts who appeared before them—often without legal representation, because there was no Free Legal Aid in the early seventies. The column was a roaring success, especially among the snobbish upper ranks of the judiciary, judges and barristers, who deplored the absence of both law and justice in the lower ranks. The legal officer class operated from the intellectual, cushy splendour of the Four Courts and looked down upon the sergeants and corporals in the trenches, the District Justices and prosecuting solicitors who fought hand to hand with the natives in the trenches.

The liberal *Irish Times* and its liberal readers loved the column too. Many an eye was wiped on many a morning in sympathy with the poor. The paper's prestige rose on the backs of the column's defence of same. One day I fell foul of a District Justice. He sued for libel on a technicality which I wanted the paper to fight. *The Irish Times*'s legal adviser and literary editor Terence de Vere White took me across to Bewley's for tea and sticky buns to explain realpolitik to me. It would be bad for *Irish Times* business to fight a libel suit against a member of the judiciary, however humble. In such a case, the judiciary would close ranks, with consequent loss to the IT of the IP—influential people.

Besides which District Justice Robert Ó hUadhaigh was really a nice fellow, a personal friend of De Vere White's, and the paper had allowed me to pound him for years. 'Deservedly,' Terence hastened to point out, but Ó hUadhaigh was getting on in years, was soon to retire, and it would be gracious to allow him one small victory over my column—a technical knockout, of course, nothing more, but some recompense for the huge gulf I had shown between Ó hUadhaigh's grasp of law and his understanding of justice and the consequent disregard in which he was held by his peers. He had also often lapsed in law also, I pointed out. All the same, De Vere said smoothly, one teensy-weensy victory for a Bridewell District Justice whom I had made the laughing stock of his superiors. An apology, no money required, De Vere had been assured in an old-boy's conversation with Ó hUadhaigh.

I refused. Editor Fergus Pyle published an apology anyway. I resigned, my union did fuck all, and I returned to the paper after a fortnight's huff. Like other union members who did not want to lose pay or jobs over me, I didn't want to lose a job either. Naturally, I was paid for my two week's absence.

I asked to be switched to the High Court and Supreme Court where the doings of their Lordships, the barristers, the white collar criminals, the business classes and the medical profession had not been adequately scrutinized. More cups of tea were taken in Bewley's. My current column dealt with lower-court hearings that lasted an average ten minutes, allowing readers a daily beginning, middle and end, including judgment and jail sentence, it was explained. The new column I proposed could take months before a conclusion was reached.

And, crucially, it was possible that the rich and powerful people upon whom I proposed to cast a beady eye would injunct or sue the paper at the drop of a hat, unlike the lower classes who did not usually read the paper and could not afford to take a libel suit.

Nor did the paper want to take on the judiciary, the builders, the doctors, or any of its ABC reading classes. The paper did not rely on income from sales—it attracted less than eighty thousand readers back then—but on in-come from advertising aimed at ABC readers with more to spend than the combined blue-collar readers of all other papers. If the IT's ABC's were to read another paper in protest against the IT's exposés of their legal shenanigans, the paper would lose lots of money.

And IT journalists would lose jobs.

So I never did get posted to the higher courts. And that's how the system worked then.

It's different now in the new climate of egalitarian Ireland. Sure who doesn't despise lawyers? And what lawyers don't despise judges? And which judges don't despise lawyers? Go to the Tribunals and have a laugh as the legal eagles tear lumps out of each other. And an even bigger laugh as the business class and politicians rip each other's intestines out in front of the judges and lawyers, assuming they can find a judge and lawyer who can bear to address each other.

Sure it's better value than the lower courts. And *The Irish Times* devotes pages and teams of journalists to it, on a daily basis. And the lawyers and judges get paid anyway, and the accused classes don't lose more than pocket money because the real profit is well stashed away offshore. And those who haven't come to the attention of the Tribunals laugh all the way to the laughing banks.

The real criminals and their IBF's whose doings in the Four Courts continue to escape scrutiny—haven't gone away. They are well protected by the punitive libel laws against which newspapers—with one eye on advertising bread and butter—have scarcely raised a whimper of protest.

FAIR SHARES

∞∞∞∞∞∞∞∞∞∞∞∞∞∞∞∞∞∞∞∞∞∞∞∞

HOT PRESS
JULY 1999

I bought shares in Telecom Eireann. It is alright for socialists to do so, said the *Marxist Review* a few years ago. Moving into the stock market is the modern way of taking control of the means of production, distribution and exchange.

In theory, those who own shares in a company, and thus have a vote, use that vote to dictate how the company operates. In practice, small shareholders are usually the minority and their votes count for little against the big cartels who own most of the shares.

That's all right. I come from a lifelong minority tradition, which was always told that its votes were useless against the big guys. Nationalist Bogside would never prevail against Unionist Stormont—but now Martin McGuinness is Minister-in-Waiting. Feminists would never win women's rights, yet we won the fight for contraception, divorce and abortion.

The vote gives the small shareholder a voice. You can go along to the annual general meeting and speak your mind and they have to listen. The moral voice has been used to good effect by minority shareholders around the globe, who raise the issue of ethical investment. Should a certain company stop investing in the arms industry? Should money be invested in organic food rather than genetically modified foodstuffs? Minority voices once revealed that the Vatican had invested in a company which had diversified into making condoms.

I haven't a clue yet what ethical issues shoud be raised at the Telecom annual general meeting. It helps that the workers there have shares in the company. They will presumably enlist our votes in pursuit of trade union demands on the company, regarding pay, working conditions and whatever. The workers themselves have a great incentive now. The better they perform, the greater the annual dividend they get on the shares, and the more their shares are worth. They will actually own the fruits of their own labour —the great Marxist dream.

Granted, their share is a minority one, and it will take a while yet for all workers to own all companies but - as Martin McGuinness might say, live horse and you'll eat grass. Right now, I'm stuffing my face. It could all come to grief, of course. Telecom faces real competition from other companies. Maybe the shares will go down in value. They could end up being worth less than we paid for them.

All the more reason to keep an eye on Telecom and its performance. Before this, we were in the comfortable position of just griping about the boss class, blaming them for every woe ever visited on the working classes—like the poor fuckers in Russia labouring under communism. Now that we shareholders are in charge, I expect there'll be a change in tune. For instance, I'm already wondering what should be done about Directory Enquiries. You dial the operator and a recorded voice tells you to join the queue, the humans will be with you soon. Time means money, and the longer I'm kept on hold, the less work I do. When I hear the recorded voice, I am listening to the sound of my Telecom investment going down the tubes. Ah yes, something must be done, as Trotsky once sighed.

Amazing, is it not? The century began with Ireland under occupation by a foreign power with not a penny of spare cash about the house. The century ends with Britain saying goodbye, the workers having a share in their own company, and the rest of us putting our money behind the workers.

Meantime, the great Essie Teelig has won an unprecedented victory down at St Ultan's flats. She refused to move out, the developers who bought the roof over her head gave in, and the Corpo is about to buy the flats for Essie and her class. Time was when the revolution was run by long-haired young ones in blue jeans. Seventy-six year old Essie in her cardigan, coat and scarf has extended the sweep and range of protest. She shouted 'Stop', and she won. Great days all round for a change.

HAUGHEY'S FALL

∞ ∞

HOT PRESS
JULY 1999

Charlie Haughey ate Brian Lenihan's liver and washed it down with Cristal champagne. Metaphorically speaking. He also consumed his son, using young Ciaran's helicopter company as a cheque machine. Whatever next? Will David Trimble hang onto the three hundred and sixty thousand quid he got for the Nobel Prize, which he promised to donate to charity? He only promised 'some' of it, a colleague points out. That's alright then. David gives thirty thousand to the Orange Widow's Benevolent Society, pockets the rest, and Charlie's his uncle. They're both 10 per cent 10 per cent to the workers and the rest to themselves. Brian got his new liver, didn't he?

Fianna Fáil and the rest of the shower in Leinster House wring their hands, draw their salaries and write substantial cheques at the taxpayer's expense to Tribunal lawyers. At Stormont, the politicians take lumps out of each other, draw their salaries and demand that London underwrites the cost of the North at the expense of taxpayers.

Well, yes and no. Some politicians should not be let out at any cost. Most of the rest lead a dog's life and money would not pay for what they have to go through. Some have paid with their lives in the North, while in both North and South many are treated like mushrooms, heaped with shit, and told to shut up.

Well, yes and no. Offhand it's difficult to think of any who walked away from it all, so the vast majority who stick it out must get some kick out of it. It can be perversely pleasant to receive a kick from a well-shod boot. You get your name and photograph in the local papers, occasionally appear in the nationals, often speak on local radio and sometimes reach the heady heights of RTE and BBC—some are never out of sight or sound.

Politicians go into orgasm as they trip over their own egos. The effect on the ego should not be underestimated. As Warhol sagely observed, everybody should be famous for fifteen minutes. Politicians, however humble, are famous for longer than that. They get photographed opening envelopes and cowsheds. They are 'tribunaled' if they open envelopes out of sight.

You don't have to join a party to be a politician. Join the Orange Order and you get a police escort. Join the picket line and your face will appear in some publication, if only in the Special Branch files. Join the women's movement and enter the archives, and get resurrected and televized as we look back over the century. Publicity is the oxygen of politics.

By and large it's still a lousy life, with little glory at the end of it. Clinton can't get laid, Haughey can't get paid any more. John Hume can't get no rest, Trimble gets no guns, Adams no government, Ahern no spouse, Quinn no majority, Bruton no luck. They'd be the first to complain about this. And the last to walk away from it.

Who would we kick if they weren't around to kick anymore? Wrong question. Since the Good Friday Agreement was signed last year, it has been an ambition of mine to walk up to each and every one of them and say, 'Thank Christ I don't have to talk to you ever again. Go and bore me no more.' Far from wanting to kick them on the political shins, I looked forward to a hush-puppy life of music, books, booze, and women's liberation. The most aggressive plan I had in mind was spraying the greenfly on the roses.

The greenfly will take an awful hammering this next month, the snails will flee for safety, the trout will feel the hook as politicians take August out. Come September and autumn, a drawing-in of the days and a touch of the night, it's back to the drawing-board again. When they do solve the North, who will be left to remember where the effing guns are stashed? Who among the current crop will be alive to remember what the row was about?

There's that at least—the politicians will die peacefully in their beds while the world rocks on, taking no notice of their passing but for a last photo and paragraph in the papers. Doubtless written by me. Journalists can be sad bastards too.

MILLENNIAL DAYS

∞ ∞

HOT PRESS
SEPTEMBER 1999

W hat a great end to the millennium. It would nearly make you believe in God and the second coming. All those guys being flushed out by tribunals and tax inspectors, and another Catholic Bishop due for a serious fall. To quote Virginia Woolf, 'There it is, then, before our eyes, the procession of the sons of educated men, ascending those pulpits, mounting those steps, passing in and out of those doors, preaching, teaching, administering justice, practising medicine, making money.'

She wrote that in the beginning of this century, when women didn't have the vote and the men who had all the power were roundly abusing it without fear of exposure. Hey, Virginia, there it is now, a procession of those same fuckers, caught with their trousers down, their hands in the cookie jar, their wigs askew, their white coats stained.

They may not be in jail—yet! But I like having them on the outside for a while longer. Put them in jail and we wouldn't have the pleasure of looking at them cringe, crawl, apologize, bluster, come out with their hands up, stand in a row before the Dáil Public Accounts Committee with their hands on the Bible.

Such delicious scenes in full colour on television, in stark black-and-white in the papers, on surround sound on the radio. These days I can't wait to wake up, turn on, tune in and listen to the naming of the bastards. The roll-call of infamy is beyond the wildest dreams of the most way out revolutionary. Then it's downstairs to turn on the telly and read the paper, the radio playing the while in the background. I've so many remote controls going, my house is like a NASA space centre. Sex, power, money, and corruption, the whole seamless web being unravelled before our eyes and ears—*Dallas* has finally come to town and J.R. Ewing is looking like an altar boy. Always liked that tune— *dah-dah, dah-DAH, dah-dah dah, dah-dah dah ....*

Bankers, judges, bishops, priests, Pro-Lifers, businessmen, industrialists. Let's be having you, boys. Are those guns in your pockets or are you just scared to death? An erection is the last thing that happens to the man who is swinging on the end of the rope, however elderly he is. I speak metaphorically of course. I don't want them dead, and not even in jail for very long. I want them out and about in the streets, the more and better and longer to enjoy the sight of them getting theirs. Huge fines will be in order of course—I want them broke. Even if we don't get them all, and we won't, money couldn't buy the spectacle.

And there's more! The Tribunals are only getting into their stride, the Bishop is still behind the fig leaf. Be still, my heart. That I should have lived to see this hour. Thank you, God, come back soon, you're welcome any time, if this is just the millennial openers. And even if there is no God, God bless Ben Dunne's cocaine habit because that's where it all began. Stay off the hard stuff, kids. No good ever came from it, as the businessmen on parade can tell you.

On top of all this, the evidence filtering out of the Derry Inquiry proves that the British government set out to have us shot dead on Bloody Sunday. I always knew it, but knowing is one thing, proving is another.

Ah, no, let's tell the truth and nothing but the truth. I never really believed that things were as bad as I said they were. How could a government have its own citizens shot?

How could bishops shag in front of the Pope? Here we approach the worst case scenario: how could the Pope not have known? How could businessmen set out to deliberately steal and cheat, wholesale and over decades? How could judges interfere with a case? How could Pro-Lifers steal babies from their mothers?

No, no, that's not right either. Any one of these individuals was capable of wrongdoing. But whole groups of them, coordinating their activities, conspiring to 'conceal the footprints,' to quote but one delicious phrase from their thesaurus? That's right up there with 'Thanks a million, big fella.' And 'Young people of Ireland, I love you.'

Times like this I wish I was an oul' wan, with nothing to do all day but traipse round the Tribunals and Inquiries, with a pocket TV and radio to hand. It's not fair, so it's not, that we working people have to put in a day's labour before we catch up on the bloodsport. Now there's a thought.

The government brought the country to a halt for three days in 1979, so that we could catch the Pope's gig. Another government-sponsored three-day standstill to watch the procession of educated men going where Virginia never thought they would go would be a nice millennium gift. God knows, working people kept the country afloat while these guys plundered the vaults and they have already paid for it, several times over.

UNDERNEATH THE CLOTH

HOT PRESS
NOVEMBER 1999

On the evidence, Archbishop John Charles McQuaid probably was homosexual. So what? If he remained celibate in accordance with his vows, his sexuality was his own private business. We are what we were born. However, many people now wonder if his homosexual orientation influenced young seminarians in his care towards homosexuality.

So what? We are all capable of changing our sexual orientation to some degree or another, and if the seminarians observed their vows of celibacy, so bloody what? Let's look at it another way. If the Archbishop was a raving heterosexual and influenced young seminarians in that direction, so what?

There's nothing wrong with heterosexuality either. A problem would arise if a homosexual was anti-heterosexual or if a heterosexual was anti-homosexual. Then we would have an inarguable case for saying such people should not be appointed to positions of power. Nobody has the right to degrade or denigrate another person's sexuality.

In the case of an Irish Catholic archbishop who controls sex education in schools and has a bias against one orientation or the other, the situation would be an affront to human rights. Nobody has the right to churn out children with prejudiced views. Of course I'm being rational here, and the furore over McQuaid is based on irrationality and sheer prejudice—against homosexuals. The people who are getting their knickers in a twist over the Archbishop are showing a subconscious loathing of homosexuality itself. That is their big problem. They want a straight priesthood. At this stage of the game, they wouldn't even mind a straight, sexually active priesthood—let the clerics have as many women as they want, but for Chrissake don't let them have men in their beds. That's what they really mean.

The argument has been obscured by the suggestion that McQuaid might have tried to get it on with young boys and that he was a paedophile. If so, people are right to be concerned. However, most people fail to distinguish between paedophilia and homosexuality. To them, it's all one and the same. A homosexual is a paedophile is a homosexual is a paedophile even though factual evidence shows paedophiles are usually heterosexual. If facts were honestly faced about priests who engage in dodgy sexual practises, it's heterosexual, not homosexual, priests we should be worrying about. Think of Father Brendan Smyth.

Then again, though most of his victims were little girls, he had a penchant for little boys too. Ah Jaysus, what we should be thinking about is how the priesthood attracts so many paedophiles, heterosexual or homosexual. Obviously, the collar gives them a perfect alibi for access to children. And beyond that again we should think about how the Catholic priesthood produces men whose sexuality has been distorted and bent out of shape. Those who enter the seminary in a perfectly healthy sexual state come out the other end as raving sexual lunatics.

How could it be otherwise when their clerical teachers, as we know from testimony about McQuaid, spent hours giving out about wanking, celibacy, and the horrible things that men and women get up to? McQuaid seems to have been obsessed about the sex act, and a dab hand at demonstrating how it was done—he formed a circle with the index finger and thumb of one hand and pushed the index finger of the other through the hole. No matter whether he was demonstrating the heterosexual or homosexual, the thought of a grown man acting like a schoolboy talking dirty about sex makes the hair stand on end. What has he and his ilk done to generations of Irish people? What are his successors doing now?

Off with their heads and their hands, and off the minds of our children and ourselves, I say, until the sexual nature of the priesthood is restored to full health. That probably means until the priesthood and the laity have equal power. It is nothing less than barbaric that the ruling caste in the Catholic Church is exclusively male. Sure, what could you expect but sexual perversion when an all-male priesthood declares women not good enough to walk with God?

SUCH LOVELY PEOPLE

∞ ∞

SUNDAY TRIBUNE
AUGUST 2000

The young man from the Czech Republic brought his guests coffee and orange juice beautifully laid out on a tray. His guests were the absentee proprietor of the Vee Valley Hotel in Clogheen, Rory O'Brien of the Clonmel Arms, and the *Sunday Tribune*. Jerry, a refugee, has made himself right at home.

As we were leaving, he and his wife were sweeping out the sun lounge of the hotel. Their five children, all under eleven in age, were playing in the garden with an African child from Nigeria and a child from Latvia. The Latvian child's mother, heavily pregnant, was examining the contents of the fridge prior to making lunch. The Nigerian mother was hanging out her washing. A married couple from Angola, here without their only daughter, had caught the bus from Cork to see other Angolan refugees.

Rory O'Brien has contravened the agreement between himself and the Directorate for Refugees and Asylum Support Seekers, DRASS, more than somewhat. He was supposed to provide a chef to cook three meals a day for the eight adults and seven children. But he takes the cheerful view that 'people aren't stupid, they can look after themselves and they prefer doing that to us doing everything for them.' DRASS says it would prefer to have been consulted about discretionary deviations; but DRASS officials haven't been down to Clogheen since the refugees were brought there on the bus a fortnight ago, acknowledges official Declan Brennan. 'We've only been up and running since last autumn,' Brennan begins excuses. No matter, and no thanks to the Department either, that the refugees and villagers among whom they live are doing so unexpectedly well together.

The village became a byword for prejudice last April when it elected a committee to oppose any refugees being sent there at all. After three weeks of uproar and a steep learning curve, the villagers opted to accept a maximum of twenty refugees in family units, and the committee reconstituted itself as a support group to welcome the new arrivals. The Department promised coeducation about the new multicultural situation into which Clogheen and the country had been plunged.

'We didn't get the promised phone call about who and how many and when they were coming,' says a disillusioned Dick Keating, cheesemaker and head of the committee. The first group arrived out of the blue one day, and that was it. Then another group arrived.' Brennan acknowledges the truth of this and adds, 'But look at who we were dealing with. Clogheen didn't want anybody.' He acknowledged the three-page information leaflet handed to the refugees in their own languages told them little about Clogheen, not even the name and number of the community welfare officer. The pages were left blank or filled with irrelevant information about faraway Clonmel, such as the names, phone numbers and addresses of the rugby club and coursing clubs.

But the refugees are blessed with the support of Linda Kennedy. Practically the first thing she did was to take the women shopping in the Clogheen supermarket. 'I let them pick their own cuts of meat and fish and used mime language to indicate the other stuff, washing-up powder and such. When we got back to the hotel there was a bit of a row. Every woman thought the stuff we'd picked up was exclusively for her. I spread the lot out on the floor and waved my arms to show it was for everybody, for as and when they needed it.'

One really lucky break for the refugees was that on the weekend following their arrival, Clogheen arranged a homecoming festival for its returning emigrants on vacation. 'We decided to go down to the hotel to bring the children out to join the treasure hunt. That night their parents went to the children's disco and everyone mixed and it was lovely and easy,' says Mary Maher, one of the festival organizers. At the invitation of Father Sean Nugent, the local people gave a standing ovation to those refugees who had come along to Mass that Sunday.

Keating describes his non-functioning committee as 'a bit like civil defence—always there when needed.' Maher says that Clogheen needs a different kind of forum now to handle the integration of locals and new immigrants. Apart from plans to take refugee families to a picnic along the riverbank under the Knockmealdown Mountains so they can see where they're living, they're not yet sure what to do. 'Everybody was exhausted after all the wrangling. One thing that will help enormously is when the kids go to school together.'

School principal Margaret Quirke has already been down to see her pupils, who speak hardly a word of English. She has promised to look into the need for an extra resource teacher for children with special needs. 'We already had the members necessary—eleven—to qualify, and now there'll be eighteen,' says Anne Keating, who divides her time as a resource teacher between three schools in the area. Clogheen is not holding its breath.

A source in the Southern Health Board, which is responsible for the health and welfare needs of the refugees, acknowledged caustically that DRASS gave them

only a few hours warning of their arrival. 'And as for trans-
lators, well, thank God for mime.' The local community
officer has arranged for the welfare to be paid by postal
cheque, and last Thursday the first weekly English lessons
for adults were held. 'They're only beginning to tell their
stories now,' says Linda Kennedy, who doesn't know where
Angola is, nor why the Republic of Czechoslovakia broke
up. Nor does Rory O'Brien. Nor does anybody questioned
in Clogheen. DRASS did not send any background, unfortunately, about the cultures or the countries refugees come
from.' 'We have refugees from one hundred and twenty
countries,' bemoans Brennan.

'We'll learn as we go along,' said O'Brien, who has
just ordered cable TV for the hotel. There is widespread
confidence that casual paid work will be found for the new
arrivals to supplement their meagre income. Local minister
Noel Davern assured one of the public meetings that many
a refugee is 'working below in Clonmel,' and confirmed the
blind-eye stance afterwards to the *Sunday Tribune*.

'We didn't know they'd be such lovely people,' a man
confided at the local bar, where one of the Czech refugees
had wandered in to buy cigarettes. He refused offers of
alcohol and jokingly mimed that he was training for the
next football match after playing for the home side during
the homecoming festival.

INIS MÓR

∞ ∞

SUNDAY TRIBUNE
JUNE 2001

The local bus leaves the square every morning at twenty minutes to nine, and does the round trip in an hour, calling at all fourteen villages. It is a great and cheap way to see Inis Mór, the biggest of the Aran Islands. Irish, their first tongue, is spoken naturally by the passengers. Even as the bus pulls out of Kilronan, there is a queue of young summer school scholars outside the supermarket. They've come to stock up on sweets, crisps and soft drinks. They are allowed into the shop in tens.

The shop is staffed by people from Latvia, who have picked up a smattering of Gaelic. The Latvians spent the winter in Rossaveal in Connemara, freezing the fish brought in by trawlers from the islands. The pier and freezing plant at Rossaveal was built in the seventies, and was the saving of the Aran islanders, who made a fortune out of herring back then.

The herring are gone as are the local lobster grounds, and now the islanders must rove out on six hundred-mile journeys now to make a living. The Latvians, working legally, many of them with degrees in agriculture, expect to have earned and saved enough from their nine-month sojourn to put a deposit on a farm back home.

The local bus is driven by a man from Yorkshire who arrived on Inis Mór two years ago in pursuit of a doomed romance, but fell in love all over again—with the people

224

and the island. The bus picks up islanders who are going to work in the co-op and the craft shops, and pensioners who are going into Kilronan for a morning's people-watching over a cup of coffee in local restaurants. The restaurants, fast food and gourmet, are staffed by teenagers who come in from the mainland for summer work. There is much to see and the pensioners travel free, of course, on the bus, as do pensioners from the mainland, who come over for the day on the CIE-subsidized boats.

These boats disgorge hundreds of passengers practically every hour. Most visitors are daytrippers. It is great crack watching them walk onto the pier and halt, confronted by a delicious choice between bicycles, sight-seeing tourist buses, and pony and trap outfits. Those who stay overnight, usually two, have a rich variety of guest houses and hotels to tempt them. Many of the landladies are island teachers making an extra living in the summer.

There is no poverty on the island now, a local says with satisfaction. Only a couple of herring millionaires, he adds quickly, the rest make do with a variety of jobs. No one job is really sufficient, says the retired lighthouse keeper. As the bus embarks on its return journey from the far end of the island, it picks up a woman beneath the great fort of Dún Aengus who waves to her husband driving his trap uphill on the journey to Kilronan. Her job started at nine-thirty and the bus is quicker than the pony and trap.

We watch a horse walk in a front door to fetch its tardy owner to work. The woman's husband wears a lovely faded pink windcheater. She will sell the handknitted Aran sweaters that men like him used to wear. The only place you'll see traditional dress now is in the interpretative centre, where you can goggle at the red flannel skirts that boys and girls alike used to wear and the gorgeous woven crios that the fishermen used to tie around their Aran sweaters, and rawhide pampooties (boots), and women's shawls. The centre is the only place where you will get a feel of how harsh and hard their lives were up until a mere thirty years ago, and for that you have to watch the ninety-minute black-and-white movie *Man Of Aran.*

Then you stumble out into sunshine, American clothes, handsome slate-roofed houses with conservatories, tarma-cadamed roads, local cars, and waves of tourists on bikes. The odd thatched cottage is still to be seen, though likely as not to be centrally heated. An open fire, dependent still on turf imported from Connemara, is a luxury, though they can afford that. Somebody will yet make a fortune from turning one of these few remaining genuine cottages into a living museum. The wonderful grey stone walls and small emerald green fields —soil and seaweed and sand were piled on the rock bed of the island to make them—are all that remain of the way Inis Mór was. They are more than worth the journey. You can feel yourself slow down as you look over the walls and watch the grass grow and animals graze and potato plants flower.

The air is fresh and clean and life-enhancing. People succumb to temptation and throw their bikes on the ground, their bodies on the greenery or the shore, and their faces to the high sky. Towards evening, the cuckoo calls and rabbits come out. Cattle low, sheep sleep, and revellers visit the pubs. High up within the oval walls of Dún Aengus, thou-sands of years old, there is no such peace. The oval is open ended. It ends at the cliff edge. You walk in through the entrance where a door might have been—the entrance, seen from below, seems like a magic or evil eye drawing you up the hill—and there is an inclination to go right to the edge, lie down and look down the length of the cruel cliff face.

The islanders used to abseil down the cliff and gather birds' eggs. Puffins and gulls and cormorants nest there. On a clear day, you can see the Cliffs of Moher on the main-land or whales or dolphins at sea. On a bad day, you will be hit in the face with spray thrown up by the waves that roar hundreds of feet below. Archaeologists are still trying to read the stones and human and animal remains found within the fort. Who could have wanted to live in a fort that has no protecting wall at the cliff edge? Beyond the fort's land-bound perimeter, thin jagged standing stones rear up like a thicket of stakes. Dún Aengus wipes the smile from your face.

The puffing holes that draw the sea hundreds of feet below ground near Kilronan would also put the fear of God in you. People made their living out of cliff faces and puffing-holes and currachs on the ocean within living memory. The haemorrhage of Aran islanders to the mainland cut the population in two in the late sixties but ceased with the building of the pier and the introduction of deep-sea trawlers and plane flights from Galway.

A thousand people live on Inis Mór now. In the early morning, as the bus sets off to bring pensioners back to Kilronan for coffee, six currachs are commissioned to row out to sea and escort a boat load of Americans to the island.

It looks like the happy opening scene from *Jaws*. Summer's here and the living is easy.

LILY

∞ ∞

NELL
2005

My mother died on Thursday, 16 December 2004, just before six in the morning. I was in Dublin. Sister Muradech called me from the Nazareth, said that my mother was 'very low,' and that she was going to send for our Carmel. I stayed in bed with the light on, very still. Twenty minutes later, Carmel phoned and said straight out that Mammy was dead. I liked that she did not attempt a preamble. My mother had woken, called out, and died quickly within minutes of heart failure, surrounded by staff.

You could say, and I do, that she died in peace.

You could say, and I do, that she and I had been very well together in the seven weeks between the launch of my book on 2 November and her death on 16 December. You could say, and I did say to her, as I gathered her corpse into my arms when I got to the Nazareth just after eleven that Thursday morning, that everything had turned out just grand.

She was clothed in a dark blue frock sprigged with white leaves, and a light blue cardigan. Her dead body, was supple and warm, a lovely surprise. I put my arms around her waist and shoulders, lifted her up, cradled her head in my hand, nestled her silvered curly head on my shoulder, buried my face in her hair, rocked her and spoke to her. I gave heartfelt thanks to her and to her God. I whispered 'Thank you' to her, and assured my dead mother that I felt just great and that there was nothing at all to worry about, that I was well at ease in myself. I was more candid and intimate than I ever had been with her while she lived.

I console myself that that's all right—that I had been reticent, to her face while she lived, just as she had been reticent to mine because there was only so much candour I could expect a woman of her generation to take on board. The playwright Pat Coby, who knew us both, wrote to me after my mother's death: 'How you carefully kept step with one another is so lovely.'

Thank you, Mammy, I said over and over in my mind. It was over. And that was best, for her, for me, and for our family.

The seven weeks between the publication of my book, and my mother's death, had been tumultuous. Hours after my book was launched at a huge reception at the Shelbourne Hotel, Carmel had told me that her husband Kevin, previously diagnosed with bowel cancer, had been given a tentative prognosis of lung cancer and a possible one year left to live. We might as well have been told that the death sentence had been passed on Carmel herself, the beating heart at the centre of our family, so close is she to Kevin and us to him.

The results of the final test were due that Thursday, 16 December, the day my mother died. My mother knew this. My mother died in the morning. In the afternoon Kevin got the all clear. 'It's all right,' we greeted mourners at the door. 'Mammy's dead, Kevin lives. It's a great bargain.'

Irrational exuberance? Yes.

Religious nonsense? Yes.

My mother held on, until all was well?

Yes?

Sure I don't know.

I only know the facts of the sequence.

Oh, joyful sequence. It was a happy wake and happy

funeral. Kevin came out of hospital for it, his six foot three frame thin and hunched.

About a week before the book launch I sank into a state of fear, recognizing that the media would initially and rightly focus on my sexual orientation. I had directed everyone to it in the opening paragraph of the book, and declared my fear of the lesbian label is in its closing page.

I talked to myself a lot before meeting the media. Would I try to broaden attention to the rest of my life—civil rights, feminism, and campaigning journalism? Yes, of course, but if I were the journalist conducting the interview, I too would focus primarily on the gay aspect, on what it was like to live a life outside the norm. I had been doing that all my life in other ways, of course. To be born Catholic in the anti-Catholic North was to live outside the norm; to be born female was outside the prevailing male norm. To live a feminist life was to live outside the male norm; to attempt socialism in a capitalist society was outside the norm; but to live a lesbian life which differed from the worldwide norm—now there was a thing of real human interest.

I had persuaded myself all the way until the eve of publication that the lesbian life was no different than any other, give or take a parent or two, a neighbour or three. And what is a lesbian life anyway? Other than loving a woman, I was a human being like any other, give or take an ideological difference or four.

So I talked to myself. And I was astonished to realize that the curse put upon me in the womb in 1944 by all religions and all societies had gone deep into me and not been exorcized. The elegant words of the Catholic Church that people like me were 'intrinsically disordered' translated into street language as 'queer'. I was queer, they said, and born with a defective gene. It is a dogma of the Catholic Church that all babies are born with the stain of original sin, and sin can only be removed by baptism. Baptism cannot change or remove genes. In 1944, the year I was born, homosexuals and lesbians were being cast into the gas ovens of Auschwitz alongside Jews and gypsies.

I thought of the curse put upon my parents because their first-born Mary Anne died within two hours of birth, unbaptized, and was consequently consigned to what the Catholic Church called limbo—an eternally suspended state between heaven and hell. Their daughter would never get to heaven though they would, and even Hitler could. My father died before the Catholic Church retracted the nonsense of limbo.

But the other curse was still upon me, and the fear of that was still in my mother. I was making her face that ghastly fact in public, plunging us both into the maelstrom.

Mammy, Mammy, I have to leave you now. I will be cursed no more. And I will do it in Derry, before the wider news breaks.

Just before the book came out I wrote an article for a local paper, *City News*, in response to a priest who had invited a woman to speak from the pulpit during Sunday Mass. She was the mother of a gay son. She spoke out about homophobia. I criticized the priest who had performed belated funeral rites for Mary Anne for not speaking from the pulpit himself about one virulent source of homophobia, the Church teaching he was bound to uphold. I declared myself a child born gay.

In their tactful way, some people in Derry mentioned that they had, 'Read your article today, Nell'.

I gave an extensive and raw interview to the local BBC radio station. It went out the day of the launch. I used the sound bite that I had worked out. 'People have seven days to call me Lesbian Nell. After that, we get back to normal and my name is Nell.' My mother didn't hear it but just about everybody else in Derry did. I got a phone call from

231

Mother Gertrude, to whom I had dedicated the book. Gentle, soothing and frail, now in her ninetieth year, she said that she heard the interview and that I was not to worry.

By the time journalists came flooding into my home, I was ready, though still nervous. Mammy, Mammy.

It helped enormously that I was interviewed at home. Apart from anything else, there is a smoking ban in all public places in Ireland. I am my parent's daughter: bring them home. I was also at ease because the young public relations expert Grainne Killeen was entertaining journalists in one room while I overshot my allocated time in another. Patsy lived in my house for that media week. The accomplished and earthy writer Evelyn Conlon, from whom I constantly take courage and inspiration, came every night. Ann came over from Canada. The company of these women lent the impression of ease and plenitude.

However, this was not at all like my real life, and the media reported on what they saw as the thrust of my book. 'The Lonely Passion of Nell McCafferty' was the headline taken from the text, printed over an article written by a journalist I like, Kathy Sheridan of *The Irish Times,* the morning of 2 November, the day of the book launch. The book resonated with a sense of exclusion, she thought.

So be it, I thought. I was a lesbian woman, living alone. Or a middle-aged sixty year-old woman, who had loved and lost, and was now alone.

Mother, mother, I can handle it but I dread meeting you. How will you handle this?

Our Muireanna, Nuala and Carmel came to the Shelbourne for the launch, with husbands and nieces and nephews. It was the first time in my life that I had allowed my family to be with me on a professional occasion. I was surprised that they had insisted on coming and surprisingly affected by their enthusiasm.

Historian and nun Margaret Mac Curtain, also known as Sister Ben, launched the book. She had extensively researched my career in journalism, books and feminism. I was dead pleased when many of those who had never heard her speak publicly asked afterwards out of respect and curiosity who this woman was?

When my turn came I said that the wound inflicted on me at birth was now healed. I declared myself finally free and untainted. Sometimes I can speak quite well. I did, that night. Hundreds of people queued to have their books signed.

The Late Late Show on 5 November began as an ordeal. Chat-show host Pat Kenny promoted me as the woman who nearly had the love affair of the century with actor Colin Farrell, by now an international superstar. I was furious that the apex of my life was deemed to be a ten-minute flirtation with a young fellow. The interview was hugely important. Sales of the book to television's biggest national audience depended on it. I knew that how I presented myself would be crucial to audience reaction. I had to choose between profit and feminist principle.

I chose principle and immediately criticized Pat on air for reducing my achievements to meeting Colin. And then I went for broke and focused the conversation on my lesbianism. I spoke directly to camera, to the parents of gay children and to gay children, who were 'sitting on sofas around the nation, sweating blood,' as I had so often sweated in my mother's home when programmers focused on homosexuality. I exhorted parents and gay children to love each other, as my parents had loved me. I asked the studio audience if they considered me born defective. They said no and there was applause. I said they had to choose between God and what the Holy Men taught, as they had once chosen between contraception and what the Holy Men taught against its use.

After the show, I asked each member of the audience as they filed out if they had known that I was lesbian? The great majority of them did not—contrary to the declaration of many journalists that of course the public knew what the media village knew.

When I went home that night there were messages on the answering machine from parents of gay children. They confirmed that it is rare in Ireland, or anywhere, for parents of gay children to be at ease and open within or outside of the family.

Next day, accompanied by Evelyn, I went to Eason's bookstore in O'Connell Street. The crowd, several hundred strong, stretched around the block. I spoke individually to every one, old and young, female and male. There were kisses and hugs and winks and handshakes and embraces. I was high and happy and overwhelmed at the palpable mood of affection.

That day unknown to me, Carmel read the opening paragraph of my book to my mother. She played a video of the *Late Late* in the nursing home's television room for my mother and other residents. Carmel says my mother nodded when I appealed to parents to love their gay children and that she murmured, 'That's right, that's what I did.'

The other Nazareth residents, whose average age was ninety, agreed, Carmel tells me. Carmel, of course, is a great professional actress, and the fiercely protective head of our family; but Sister Muradech approved the showing of the video and it is her job to ensure that residents don't die of heart attack from cultural shock.

On Monday I went to Derry and brought my mother home from the Nazareth. She asked how my book was selling. Grand, I said. I was nervous. Next day, on her ninety-fourth birthday, the neighbours arrived. They each had a birthday present for my mother in one hand and a copy of my book in the other. 'You were great on the *Late*

Late,' was the smiling, discreet comment. I was home and dry. The neighbours were aged seventy and upwards. Many of their adult children made the journey to Beechwood Street.

My mother was happy and proud, both of her own great age and of the congratulations being showered on me. It was a glorious day. All the trials of all my life were over. It didn't matter what else might happen—my mammy and the neighbours and I were at home with each other.

On 13 November I went to sign books at the Derry branch of Eason's. It was stunning. I spent hours with hundreds of people from my native city. I cannot explain it. The week ended as it had begun, book-ended by related and unforeseen coincidences. On 8 November two women had successfully applied in the High Court for leave to take a judicial review of the Revenue Commissioner's decision not to recognize their Canadian marriage. Katherine Zappone is former head of the Irish Council for the Status of Women. Her partner Ann Louise Gillligan sits on the Irish Human Rights Board. On Sunday, 14 November, Taoiseach Bertie Ahern supported the concept of civil union for gay couples. The Catholic Archbishop of Dublin, Diarmuid Martin, assented to this view.

At the end of November, the Nazareth sent for us all. My mother's health was very low. I spent two nights sleeping on the floor beside her bed, wrapped in a duvet. Sometimes I slept right through the staff's ministrations to her. Sister Muradech made it as easy as she could when asking us to select an undertaker. Carmel and I went personally to the undertaker's warehouse and selected the least heavy coffin from the stacked shelves. The undertaker helped us lift it experimentally on our shoulders. Carmel dryly wondered if next year we would be picking a coffin for Kevin. He was suffering many setbacks in hospital, after his operation for bowel cancer. We might have been picking out furniture. The place smelled of fresh wood. We were there about ten minutes. We hardly spoke on the car journey afterwards. Carmel went to hospital and I returned to the Nazareth. We told nobody else about it. It felt like the family was imploding. I cancelled appointments in Dublin.

On the third morning my mother woke up and said she wanted to go home. I brought her home to die. She slept soundly around the clock for thirteen days in Beechwood Street, waking only for meals and to go to the toilet. One night she was awfully pale and I put my hand over her heart and it was jumping. I decided not to call Carmel away from her vigil over Kevin in hospital. I didn't waken Nuala. I didn't call a doctor. I climbed into bed alongside her, and put my arms round my mother. Without waking, she nestled her head on my shoulder. Was this how she had nestled me when I was a sick child?

It was peaceful. It was terrifying. I was incredibly brave. In the dark, I prayed silently to her God, kept my hand over her heart, kissed her forehead. I fell asleep. Hours later I awoke to her impatient voice. 'For God's sake, Nell, this bed is very narrow. Would you not sleep on the floor, daughter?' The comeback kid was very much alive.

She was hugely entertained when the cop who ranks third in Northern Ireland, Assistant Chief Constable Peter Sheridan, called to the house to have several books signed. It was the first time since 1968 that a police officer had come into the house on a peaceful mission. She insisted that I give him a bowl of the soup sent over by Peggy McGuinness. 'Martin's mother,' she pointed out. She raised a finger to the photograph of 'good cop' Sergeant Duffy.

Peter used a screwdriver to fix the loose wires on her alarm buzzer and made it work again. Two days later, in the company of Tony Blair at Downing Street, when Martin McGuinness and Gerry Adams had their first formal meeting with the head of the Northern Ireland police chief

Hugh Orde, Peter mentioned to Martin that his mother made great soup. Martin rang his mother from Number Ten Downing Street. 'It's me and Gerry who are supposed to be dealing with the cops, not you and Lily.'

The last days of my mother's reign in her own house were ghastly. Her legs had lost their power altogether. In the short stumble between hoisting her from bed to commode, from commode to bed, her feet got tangled, her dead weight sank from my arms, and I had to lower her on four occasions to the floor. I had to cover her with a blanket, put a pillow under her head, leave her alone in her terror, and go out into the street for help.

The first time it was after midnight, no doors were open, no hall lights were on. I rang Teresa and she came down the street in her nightie. Another evening after taking her to the bathroom, we failed again in the transition from toilet seat to wheelchair, and Nuala fetched a seventeen year-old schoolboy who was frightened of being 'rough' with her. My mother was perched precariously on my buckling knee, inches from the floor.

The boy said 'Sorry, Mrs McCafferty' and we hauled her up, roughly onto the wheelchair. One evening early, as Teresa arrived yet again and we lifted her from the floor to the commode, my mother bent over, her bum went up in the air, diarrhoea unexpectedly shot out of her and up my bare arm. We got her onto the commode and she started vomiting. I retched and was fearful that the knowledge of this would humiliate my mother. She did not notice. She was nearly unconscious. Teresa sent me out of the room.

I was not there on Saturday, 4 December, when my mother fell for the last time. I had gone to the funeral of her nephew and my cousin, IRA volunteer Hugh Duffy. The Catholic Church had refused to admit his coffin into the chapel if it was draped in a tricolour. Hugh had left instructions that in such an event his body was to be buried from

237

home with beret, gloves and tricolour on his coffin, and this was done. My mother instructed me to leave her and follow his hearse.

When I arrived home Nuala was weeping over my mother's bed. The great strength of Marian, the house-keeper who came twice a week, was of no avail and my mother lay on the floor by the commode while one of Marian's relatives, summoned by phone, rushed down by car. The tension and fear in our house was crushing Nuala. A succession of neighbours said quietly that Nuala was looking poorly, and I was looking exhausted, that I could not go on, that my mother would understand. I accepted defeat, rang the Nazareth House on Monday, 7 December, and told them that I could not look after my mother at home any more.

I told her that she was just going back to the Nazareth until her legs got strong again and went to Dublin to do some interviews. I returned to Derry early on Thursday morning, 9 December, from where I emailed my friends Karen and Barbara in New York, who had tracked down the newspaper cuttings on Uncle Brian.

'Lily lies in state in Nazareth, sleeping her life away. I go up there today, bringing loads of books, to sit with her until the end. I may be there of a night, depending on Lily's state. Nuala has slightly recovered in the absence of the living horror of Lily at home. Lily will be home no more. No more, quoth the raven, nevermore. Carmel points out that we have at least solved the problem of Christmas dinner. She and her children will have it in the hospital can-teen; Nuala and I would have it in the Nazareth. If Lily is dead by then, I will take Nuala to a hotel for dinner. Cata-strophe, catastrophe.'

The Nazareth fed us morning, noon, and night, and on Tuesday evening, 14 December, Mammy woke up and decided to get out of bed and go downstairs to the Christmas party. Mr Keyes, the plumber who serviced her house in Beechwood Street, led his band through a series of swing numbers. My mother lifted her feet up and down on the pedals of her wheelchair, in time to the beat.

'Look, I can move my legs,' she said.

'I'll bring you home when I come back from Dublin on Thursday,' I said.

'For Christmas,' she nodded.

'Until after the New Year. For the full fortnight,' I said.

Such a smile that woman has when she is delighted about something.

I gave my car keys to Muradech, put my head into the brandy, put our Nuala out of my mind, joined with my mother in the great Christmas hymns, and danced the night away.

On Wednesday I woke my mother from her sound sleep in Nazareth, and reiterated that I'd be back from Dublin next day. Great party, I said. The staff has been talking about it all morning, she flashed that lovely grin. Home tomorrow, I said. Such another grin my mother gave.

The Nazareth staff lined the steps of the nursing home as we carried her out in the coffin, on Thursday afternoon, 16 December. Her death was announced on radio north and south. Just before six that evening Kevin's consultant rang. Carmel doubled over as she listened. She was crying. She was smiling. Kevin had got the all clear, she looked up and told us, and she bent over again. Kevin lives. Carmel rushed to the bathroom and threw up. Happy house. Oh happy, happy, house.

I stayed in the sitting room for the whole wake beside my mother. I slept on the floor beside her coffin, intently, selfishly devoted to my remaining time with her, two days and nights and one last morning. I was acutely aware of the steady accretion of small kindnesses from home and abroad, from friends and neighbours. The young man who recalled boyhood days visiting with my mother's grandson Paul delighted me. 'I always felt safe here. Your mother stood in the doorway of the scullery, teasing us, asking us questions.'

Though other members of her family sent condolences, Nuala Ó Faoláin did not salute the passing of my mother. I heard from a friend of a friend that she was 'angry' with my book. Still, she should have risen above our situation, I thought, and then I thought of how I had not risen properly to the passing of her own mother. Then I thought of how in her second memoir *Almost There*, Nuala had fantasized about walking away from her mother. She was now brusquely walking away from both our mothers. Ah, well.

The young parish priest, whom none of us knew, refused to let Carmel speak from the altar in tribute to Lily. Next thing, he said, the IRA would want to speak during Mass about volunteers. He had met my mother and could well speak of her, he said. Did he know about Mary Anne, I asked?

'You are tough,' he said.

'You haven't met Carmel,' I said.

Carmel said matter of factly that she would read the lesson from the altar, as the priest suggested, and then make a speech about Lily. 'What will you do, father? Stop the Mass, and throw us out?'

Later, he said Carmel could speak before Mass began.

'Will Nell be writing the speech?' he asked.

'Who is Nell?' Carmel asked?

'Can I read your speech beforehand?' he asked Carmel.

'I'm dyslexic. I can hardly read or write,' Carmel exaggerated.

The heavy coffin made me anxious as we moved down the street. None of us six women had ever carried one before. Muireanna and Carmel and I represented Lily's children. Hugh's daughter Jacqueline represented the grandchildren and great grandchildren. Teresa Cooley represented the street. Grainne McCafferty represented the friends of the family. It was a grand walk through the Bogside. The weather was fine and crisp and bright. The cortège paused where Sergeant Duffy's barracks had once been. Carmel said from the altar that all her children had crucified Lily with their troubles and that she had carried us all through them. She named us one by one and the especial characteristics Lily had noted in each. 'Nell, her lesbian daughter,' Carmel said. I burst out laughing.

Carmel ended her tribute with a smiling, whispered 'Lily, *tiocfaidh ár lá*' (our day will come), the republican aspiration for a return of the United Ireland into which our mother had been born.

During the Mass the glorious Derry soprano, Maureen Hegarty, sang hymns from long ago, Catholic and Protestant, accompanied by the organist. 'Bring Flowers of the Rarest', 'Oh Mother! I Could Weep for Mirth,' 'Nearer My God to Thee'. We relaxed into the timbred soar of her voice and enjoyed the Mass for our mother. We carried Lily out of the Long Tower church to the rousing strains of the anthem to Derry's patron saint, Saint Columba. I sang along, delighted and proud.

Kevin collapsed temporarily and we milled about outside while Carmel and the former Bishop, Edward Daly, saw him into the presbytery. All the nuns who had taught us were there. Though I remember that I remember little else. There was a grand walk through the Brandywell—an exact reverse of the 1972 Bloody Sunday route—and up into the beautiful cemetery to where our father's grave had been opened. After Lily's coffin was lowered, the Armagh piper Fintan Vallely played laments while the gravediggers completely filled in the deep hole by pre-arrangement. I had never wanted to walk away, leaving Lily in an uncovered coffin. We threw lilies in as the earth layered over her.

Lily had left money in the bank and Credit Union. We spent as much of it as we could at a lunch in the City Hotel, overlooking the River Foyle. There was an open bar. Fintan played. Evelyn sang the first song; the young followed with 'A Fairytale of New York,' and after that we all took turns. My brother Paddy sat on my knee. Emma's first born, Mammy's latest great-grandchild, two months old and over from London, was passed around. One of the teenage boys waltzed with me. Maurice gave me my first jiving lesson—in the hands of an expert teacher, it's dead easy. We went back to Beechwood Street around nine that night. I woke up feeling alien in the house and in Derry.

The book stayed in the bestseller list over Christmas. It pleased my fancy that it was considered a suitable gift for reading during celebrations of the Holy Family. Within weeks, a tooth had fallen out and my mouth was covered in cold sores. Mother Gertrude held my hands and asked me what I wanted for myself? I truly did not know. She said she believed in 'the three effs: faith, family and friends'. I told her I believed in 'eff all'. She allowed herself and me a smile.

I do not yet know what to do with freedom. I am lethargic; I sleep badly. I feel old of body, which shocks and dismays me.

I play CDs recorded by Maureen Hegarty over and over. After all those years of looking after Lily, at least I am listening to music again. Margaret Mac Curtain, does not ask, 'How are you doing?' She asks, 'How does your garden grow?'

I forgot to plant bulbs in the last autumn of my mother's life. The garden of my Dublin home in the first months of 2005 was fallow, bare earth. I know there are green things underneath. The weeds may yet be wild flowers. We shall see.

The only thing I am sure of is that I am at total ease in my metaphorical skin. Normal heartaches apart, there is no shadow over my life, because the book and its aftermath came out in my mother's lifetime. I will not die wondering. That is pure wonderful.

NOTES AND SOURCES

∞ ∞

P 15 Number Seven, *The Irish Times* 26 January 1970
Nell's first published piece for *The Irish Times* was this one about the informal and wel-
coming McClenaghan household at 7 Wellington Street, a home from home for all
passing journalists covering the Troubles. In her account, a high-up visiting Fianna Fáil
politician tips the 'boy with a beard in the Bogside' fifty pounds 'for propaganda purposes,' and writer Eamonn McCann spends it on a lefty publication attacking Taoiseach
Jack Lynch and his party. The politician was Minister Neil Blaney, Nell later disclosed,
the man dismissed from Jack Lynch's Cabinet with Charles Haughey for his part in the
arms scandal, when aid funds were diverted into arms funds.

By the late sixties the cause of civil rights had taken over the North, adding
marches and demonstrations by students and the Catholic minority—and both—to the
world's headlines about Vietnam and Cuba. Together with Nell herself, Derry's nationalists were the vanguard of the civil rights marches, with McCann, Ivan Cooper, Bernadette
Devlin and Nell herself sometimes flanking visiting sympathisers like Vanessa Redgrave,
Robert Lowell, and international supporters.

Nell's inside view of the North caught *The Irish Times* news editor Donal Foley's
eye. At the prompting of the UK *Observer's* correspondent Mary Holland, he summoned
Nell south for a job interview. According to the 'Women First' page editor Mary Maher,
the interview took place in the tiny cubicle off the newsroom where the TV was kept. 'But
Donal couldn't understand her accent, so guess who he called in to act as interpreter? The
girl from Chicago,' remembers Maher.

A year and a half later, Jack Lynch was setting up field hospitals and barracks
accommodation south of the border for northerners fleeing sectarianism and army
patrols. Two years after this piece appeared, Glenfadda Park became the scene of the 1972
Blood Sunday massacre where six victim marchers were shot dead by the British Army.

P 19 A Day I Spent with Paisley, *The Irish Times* 16 April 1970
Followers of the Reverend Ian Paisley's 'Frees' were grass-roots working-class, barely
richer than their nationalist counterparts if at all, yet anti-Catholic in the Calvinist tradition. His 'Free' Presbyterian Church of Ulster broke away from the Irish Presbyterian
Church in the 1950s. In 1970 he entered mainstream politics, forming his own breakaway
hard-line Democratic Unionist Party and running for Westminster. Paisley had preached
anti-Catholic doctrine for most of the sixties, warning the increasingly nervous and god-
fearing majority of the dangers they faced from encroaching hordes of papists. Meanwhile, the advancing nationalist armies he preached against so vehemently had acquired
free third-level education under Harold Wilson's British Labour government (it arrived
with the Welfare State in 1947) and their inspiration from the martyrs of Alabama and
Sharpeville, led by charismatic figures like Angela Davis and James Baldwin.

P 24 Our Street, 'Women First', *The Irish Times* 5 May 1970
Eddie McAteer was the Nationalist Party MP for Mid-Derry until he lost his seat to
SDLP leader and Bogsider John Hume. Nell wrote another 1970 Derry piece, 'A Bathroom in the Bogside,' now lost, when her Beechwood Street home became one of few to
acquire a bathroom and indoor toilet in the Bogside. These were the first pieces of their
kind to appear in the southern Irish press, for whom the North of either tradition had hitherto been a closed book.

P 28 Her Majesty's Derry, *The Irish Times* 2 December 1970
The history of Derry as a garrison town goes back four centuries and originated with
Tyrone's chieftain, Hugh the 'Great O'Neill', and his rebellion against Queen Elizabeth
the First. When Derry's naval base closed in June 1969, the city suffered a sizeable economic blow. It also sustained a heavy loss in visiting foreign sailors whose ships docked
regularly at Derry during NATO exercises: 'Consequently ... it is a pleasure to be wined
and dined without regard to the 'Buroo Budget.' Nell was referring to national assistance
or dole money. 'But the relationship broke down when British soldiers pointed guns at
the population after 1969,' she adds now.

P 30 My Mother's Money, 'Women First', *The Irish Times* 1 March 1971
The historic UK currency of pounds, shillings and pence disappeared on 15 February
1971 both north and south of the border. Ireland decimalized its punteanna at the same
time as the UK, dividing it as the UK did into 100 pennies or pingin. That currency was
replaced on 1 January 2002 by the Euro.

P 32 Derry's Soldier Dolls, *The Irish Times* 15 November 1971
On 14 August 1971 the British introduced internment without trial. The Bogside's welcome mat for British troops vanished overnight and army-civilian relations deteriorated
fast. Catholic community refugees from places like Portadown began to flood makeshift
camps and hospitals south of the border, fleeing sectarian hostilities and an increasingly
heavy army presence. The previous year the IRA had split between the left-leaning Official IRA (or 'Stickies', in reference to the self-adhesive Easter lily lapel badges) and
exclusively pro-armed struggle Provisional IRA ('Provos'). The Official IRA was subsequently disbanded in Derry. On 10 November two Derry girls were tarred and feathered.
Soon after Nell's first cousin, herself engaged to marry a British soldier, was also tarred
and feathered.

P 40 Coat Tales, 'Women First', *The Irish Times* 24 December 1971
From a very popular 'Women First' all-star Christmas feature called 'All Our Yesterdays'
which also had pieces by Maeve Binchy and Gabrielle Williams. 'Women First' was the
women's page of *The Irish Times,* launched by Donal Foley and Mary Maher, and later
edited by Maeve Binchy and Christina Murphy. By the late seventies women writers had
been absorbed into the rest of the paper; current editor Geraldine Kennedy is a graduate
of those later days.

P 44 Numbed and Restless, *The Irish Times* 2 February 1972
Of the 3630 violent deaths recorded in the Northern Ireland Troubles, none caused more
public shock and outrage than those of the thirteen men and boys shot by British paratroopers during the anti-interment civil rights demonstration in the Bogside on 30 January 1972, the day which forever after became known as 'Bloody Sunday.' Nell delivered

the first eye-witness account, 'Three Men Die on the Barricades,' dated 31 January 1972. This is her second piece from the following day. The male victims had been peaceful protesters and were not carrying weapons. The universal outcry that followed the twenty minutes of gunfire the army turned on the unarmed marchers resulted, thirty years later, in the public inquiry convened by British Prime Minister Tony Blair under Lord Saville.

Former British leader and Tory chief Sir Ted Heath was among the hundreds of witnesses called in to testify to the Saville Inquiry in Derry's Guildhall, which became the stage for many weeks of testimony. Witnesses were also heard in a London secure setting, where paratroopers testified anonymously, claiming they would be endangered by appearing in the Northern Irish city.

P 47 Disruption Day, *The Irish Times* 9 February 1972
A no-go area for British troops, the Nationalist enclave known as Free Derry centered on the Bogside Inn and circumscribed the Bogside and Brandywell within a series of homemade barricades. Run by citizens' committees, it organized strike days, classes, and more. Its homemade security system began with the giant message, 'You are now entering Free Derry Corner', and murals painted by the Bogside artists, originally the gable wall of the Lecky Road end house where civil rights demonstrations and public meetings were held. British soldiers drove an armoured vehicle to topple it but local people have resisted all efforts to remove it.

P 51 Martin McGuinness: Profile of a Provo, *The Irish Times* 19 April 1972
When internment was introduced in August 1970 Martin McGuinness was still a quiet teenager unused to the public gaze. But by 1971 the eighteen year-old stone thrower of 1969 had become Officer Commanding of the 'Free Derry' Provisional IRA, and had appeared at a Provisional IRA press conference where the new leadership offered peace talks. This profile was not only the first published with McGuinness, but the only interview in which he discussed his role and feelings as an IRA volunteer—an enduring testament to the unusual access McCafferty had to her Bogside neighbours.

In May 2001 McGuinness confirmed to the Saville Inquiry that at the time of the Bloody Sunday killings that he was second-in-command of the IRA in the city. He vehemently denied allegations that he had fired the first shot and called claims that he had fired on soldiers 'lunatic'. Six republican witnesses refuted accusations that he had planned to use a nail bomb that day. His first meeting with British politicians came in July 1972, when the Provisional leadership was secretly taken to London for what would turn out to be failed talks with the British government. He was still only twenty-one at the time. During the seventies McGuinness avoided internment—but not a conviction and four-year prison sentence for terrorism-related offences south of the border, a year after this appeared.

P 56 Village in the Mountains, *The Irish Times* 22 June 1972
Originally published as one in a series of pieces written around southern France, under the rubric 'A Day in the Life of a Basque Village,' this heralded *The Irish Times* expansion into Europe, starting with France and the arrival of newly appointed (and much loved) Paris editor Fergus Pyle, now replaced by Lara Marlowe.

P 62 In the Eyes of the Law, 1973-1977
This is the introduction to the 1981 Ward River Press book of the series from *The Irish Times* and was the first of Nell's paperback collected editions.

P 65 Persistent Maoist Taken to Cells, 'In the Eyes of the Law', *The Irish Times* 25 May
1973
Led by jailed former Trinity College Dublin student David Vipond, Maoists and courts
were a familiar combination in the early seventies.

P 71 Bells and Smells, 'In the Eyes of the Law', *The Irish Times* 12 June 1973
The Hare Krishnas were the most visible of several cults to arrive and thrive around
Dublin then.

P 76 Sex Offender, 'In the Eyes of the Law', *The Irish Times* 24 January 1974
In this case the sinner did sin again forthwith despite the lenience and clemency of the
judge, it was later disclosed.

P 79 Has She A Black Eye or Anything? 'In the Eyes of the Law', *The Irish Times* 29
July 1974
Marital disputes, once known as 'conjugals' to Dublin gardaí, were a frequent theme of
the series.

P 81 Consenting Adults, *'In the Eyes of the Law', The Irish Times* 12 September 1975
When this testimony about a very common sexual act was published in Nell's 'Eyes of
the Law' column, a massive press silence was broken by the subject matter. Although certain Dublin bars and haunts were known to 'the love that dares not speak its name,' and
some Dublin figures led double lives, public and private, straight and gay, *The Irish Times*
was first to print a frank account.
    Shortly after reading a courageous paper calling for equal gay rights at Trinity
College Historical Society, future President Mary Robinson helped start a campaign for
the decriminalization of homosexuality during the 1970s with legal and academic comrades. The campaign's most public figure was David Norris, prominent Joycean and
Trinity College lecturer, who was also founder of the Hirschfeld Centre and a senator in
Seanad Éireann, the Irish Senate. The campaign to legalize homosexuality ended at the
Court of Human Rights in Strasbourg and was aided by legal advisors Garret Cooney and
Mary McAleese; the future president was then the Reid Professor of Law at Trinity College Dublin. She was also, ironically, advisor to the Irish Roman Catholic Bishops and
was elected President of Ireland in 1997.
    Homosexual acts remained officially illegal in Ireland up until the summer of
1993 when Taoiseach Albert Reynolds and the Fianna Fáil/Labour government lifted the
Offences Against the Person ban, and declared the age of consent to be seventeen, the
same as that for heterosexuals. The age of consent for lesbians and oral acts has since
been lowered to fifteen.

P 84 Armagh Is a Feminist Issue, *The Irish Times* 17 June 1980
After her 'Armagh Jail' piece was published in 1980, Nell wrote one attacking male chauvinism within trades unions. She resigned when this was not carried in *The Irish Times*
and went over to *Magill* magazine, whose editor Vincent Browne had offered her as much
space as she needed. It marked the beginning of a long career at *Magill,* where length was
never a problem. 'Gilmour' is trimmed in this version, but is far from being her longest
piece there—her 1986 'Peace People At War' was over 12,000 words, well on the way to
book-dom and too long for this collection.
    When Nell left *The Irish Times,* Irish Writers' Co-Op brought out her *Armagh*

Women, and Ward River Press published the collected columns from her 'In the Eyes of the Law' series. Her popular contributions to *In Dublin* and *Magill* were accompanied by an irreverent feminist RTE radio commentary, followed by a more irreverent TV commentary focusing on male chauvinism in the media. She subsequently started writing a syndicated column for *Kerry's Eye,* London's *Spare Rib* and *Out* magazines. 'I worked for anyone who commissioned me.'

P 89   School Was Never Like This, *Irish Press* 24 July 1981
The Merriman Summer School was the very happy playground of media figures and the Dublin chattering classes for many a year throughout the seventies and beyond—and still is.

P 93   The Accusing Finger of a Derry Supergrass, *Magill* April 1983
Known in the popular press as the Derry 'supergrass,' Raymond Gilmour was an Irish National Liberation Army volunteer who was prosecuted for robbing a Post Office, for which he received the unusual punishment of a suspended sentence. He later joined the Provisionals then turned himself in to the British army as a 'Gyppo Nolan'-style informer (a character immortalized by Victor McLaglan in Liam O'Flaherty's 1925 novel). He was by no means the only supergrass, but he was far and away the most effective, despised, and also most charming and persuasive—or so his victims avowed.

P 105   Referendum, Part One *In Dublin* April 1983
There have been five Irish referenda on abortion in the past twenty years. In 1983 the people voted to insert an amendment into the constitution giving equal rights to life to the pregnant mother and unborn child. But in 1992 the Irish Supreme Court ruled that a suicidal fourteen-year-old rape victim, known as X, was entitled to a termination in Ireland. She had to travel to England when subsequent Irish governments failed to legislate for the Supreme Court ruling thus putting sympathetic doctors at risk of prosecution. The 2002 referendum was as passionate, divisive and expensive as the 1983 one, and it attempted to overrule the X ruling. Pro-life groups have long campaigned against the X ruling and the 2002 referendum is the latest attempt to overturn it. Around 7000 women travel to England for abortion annually, though this is an approximate figure. Abortion is, of course, still illegal in the South and still available in England despite various Supreme Court decisions following the 'X' case.

P 121   Bishop Casey: As Sexual as Anyone Else, *In Dublin* June 1984
The former bishop of Kerry and Galway resigned in 1992, after his relationship with American divorcee Annie Murphy became public, along with his child from that union. His relationship had begun in 1973 according to Ms Murphy's account. The bishop went to Mexico and Ecuador before settling down in a parish near Gatwick, but did not return to his Irish parochial duties.

P 127   The Kerry Babies, 'The Opinions of Mighty Medical Men', *Irish Press* 15 March 1985
The Inquiry into the Kerry Babies case lasted for nine months and became an unprecedented show of legal and judicial cruelty as the court probed intimate details of Joanne Hayes to determine exactly how the police had wrongfully charged her with giving birth to two babies by two different men, and then killing them at different ends of County Kerry, with the collusion of her own family members. Nell's accounts of the trial appeared in the columns of the *Irish Press. Woman to Blame* is Nell's paperback summary of the

Joanne Hayes case and the inquiry known as the Kerry Babies. The book was not carried by Eason's bookstore chain, reportedly from a fear of libel suits. Ironically, three other titles on the Inquiry that Eason's did carry were successfully sued for libel, while Nell's was not. Hayes was inundated with daffodils during the inquiry, thousands of flowers being sent to her courtroom after Nell's personal appeal. The alleged double infanticide in the Kingdom coincided with the phenomenon of the 'Moving Statues' that gripped all of Ireland in the summer of 1985 while Nell was writing her book about the court case.

P 132 Little Richard, *Out magazine number three* January-April 1985
The 'Georgia Peach' appeared in *The Girl Can't Help It,* a 1956 film starring the well-endowed Jayne Mansfield, and this piece appeared just after he came out—as a Minister.

P 142 The Man Who Fell to Earth, 'Pope Revisited', *In Dublin* 17 April 1986
The Pope's late September visit to Ireland was, of course, seven years earlier than this piece. Nothing negative appeared in Irish newspapers around the visit, despite a sudden hardening of the papal line on contraception and sex. So Nell is probably the only writer to have captured the sudden downwards swoop in public mood after the first, very heady day in Phoenix Park.

P 146 Chernobyl: Sentence of Death, *Kerry's Eye* 1 May 1986
On 25 April in 1986 the worst nuclear power accident to date happened at Chernobyl in the former USSR, in what is now Ukraine. The Chernobyl nuclear power plant was located eighty miles north of Kiev and had four reactors; whilst testing reactor number four, certain safety procedures were disregarded. At 1:23 am the chain reaction in the reactor ran out of control, creating explosions and a fireball that blew off the reactor's massive steel and cement lid. The Chernobyl accident killed more than thirty people immediately, hundreds in the aftermath and countless thousands in the long term who suffered from radiation poisoning as a result of the high radiation levels in the surrounding twenty-mile radius. 135,000 people had to be evacuated. The number of victims is now put at 70,000, but is more or less incalculable.

P 152 The Life and Death Mary Norris, *Irish Press* 16 July 1986
This version is shortened, of necessity.

P 160 Divorce: Split Happens, *Hot Press* 3 May 1995
For half of the twentieth century there was no divorce in Ireland. On Friday 24 November 1995, a million plus Irish voters decided at last in favour of lifting the ban on divorce introduced by then leader Éamon De Valera. Thanks to a strongly urban turn-out, the Irish people voted 'yes' to divorce this time in a new referendum with the slimmest of margins. Under President Éamon de Valera, Article 41.3.2 of his 1937 Constitution Bunreacht na hÉireann had passed in 1937, stating that no law could provide for the grant of dissolution of marriage. Half a century later in 1986, a referendum to remove this divorce ban was roundly defeated. The 'Yes' vote was 36.5 per cent in an acrimonious campaign, during which North Dublin TD Alice Glenn stated that 'women voting for divorce would be like turkeys voting for Christmas'.

P 164 Sarajevo Siege, *Sunday Tribune* 15 August 1995
The final days of the Bosnian War stand-off as reported from inside the walls. When Sarajevo was elected to host the 1984 Winter Olympics, the euphoria of the games and a

good economy was the opposite of what was to come less than a decade later. On 6 April 1992 Sarajevo was besieged by Bosnian Serbs. The ensuing war ended in destruction and loss of population. Reconstruction started in 1995. By 2003 most of the city was rebuilt, with the development of the ''Bosmal City Centre' by the Bosnian Malaysian firm of the same name featuring the tallest building in the Balkans. Sarajevo has launched more bids to host numerous Winter Olympics.

P 169 Veronica Guerin, *Hot Press* 11 July 1996
When the admired and respected crime reporter Veronica Guerin was gunned down on the outskirts of Dublin in June 1996 she became a sort of latter-day Irish saint. For two years the *Sunday Independent* reporter and former accountant had mounted an audacious, headline-grabbing campaign against Ireland's drug warlords in the headlines of the newspaper. Her murder was greeted with horror and revulsion by her fellow journalists. Her murder stunned the media and the government, the public came out at her funeral in thousands, and books and a film followed. Radical and successful legislation was immediately introduced to confiscate the profits of crime through the Criminal Assets Bureau.

P 176 Farewell to Robbo, *Hot Press* 4 September 1997
Mary Robinson was the first woman President of Ireland from 1990 to 1997, and then resigned a year early to serve as the United Nations High Commissioner for Human Rights from 1997 to 2002. Raised in Ballina, County Mayo, as a doctor couple's daughter, she was among the first Catholics to enter Protestant Trinity College; at a time when Catholics were urged to kiss the Archbishop McQuaid's ring and ask permission. She went in to study law and to become a barrister with a firm agenda of reform. After being elected the first woman head of the Trinity College 'Hist' Society, she campaigned on behalf of civil, gay, and reproductive rights as an academic, barrister and member of the Irish senate (1969-1989). As a candidate of the Labour Party in the 1990 presidential election, she defeated Fianna Fáil's Tánaiste Brian Lenihan and became the first elected non-Fianna Fáil president, as well as the first woman president. After Robinson resigned the presidency for the United Nations post, her work on behalf of human rights in Sierra Leone, East Timor, the West Bank and the Sudan shed light on the plight of African child soldiers and their victims amongst other horrors. Since 2002 she has served as the Honorary President of Oxfam International and she is a founding member and Chair of the Council of Women World Leaders. Her newest project is the Ethical Globalization Initiative (EGI), which seeks to establish human rights as part of the globalization process in developing countries. Since 2004 she has also taught international human rights law as Professor of Practice in International Affairs at Columbia University in New York.

P 179 Race for Áras, *Hot Press* 2 October 1997
The second presidential race featured four women candidates and a man, Derek Nally. The former Irish news journalist and Queens University Belfast Vice-Chancellor Mary McAleese went on to become the eleventh Republic of Ireland president as the Fianna Fáil candidate. In close second place was Mary Banotti, the Fine Gael nominee and grand-niece of the hero and rebel of the war of independence, Michael Collins. The Chernobyl childrens' fund campaigner Adi Roche was the Labour Party choice and Eurovision Song Contest winner Dana from Derry made fourth.

P 182 Free Winnie, *Sunday Tribune* 30 November 1997
The former wife of South African leader Nelson Mandela emerged as a leading opponent

of the white minority government during the last part of her husband's twenty-eight years of hard labour as a prisoner on Robben Island (August 1962 to February 1990). For many of those years she was exiled to the town of Brandfort in the Orange Free State and infrequently permitted to visit her husband there. As a respected, jail 'widow' she was known as 'the Mother of the Nation.' She was an educated nurse, while he was educated royalty. Her reputation was grievously injured by a reckless and infamous speech in defence of the anti-apartheid struggle that she gave at Munsieville, supporting the practice of 'necklacing,' or burning victims to death with flaming tyres. On 13 April 1985 Mrs Mandela said, 'with our boxes of matches and our necklaces we shall liberate this country.'

Further injurious to her name and character was her association with the January 1989 kidnapping and murder by her bodyguards of a fourteen year-old ANC activist called Stompie Seipei Moketsi. In 1991 she was convicted of his abduction, and of being a collaborator by association in his death. She narrowly avoided jail when her six-year sentence was reduced to a fine on appeal. Mandela separated from his wife of thirty-eight years in April 1992, and they divorced in March 1996. During the post-apartheid era, Winnie allied herself far less than her former husband in the cause of peace and reconciliation with the white former oppressors, as this account of her long-running trial makes plain.

P 188 Mo Mowlam, *Hot Press* 14 May 1998
Mo (Marjorie) Mowlam served in Tony Blair's Cabinet as Minister of State for Northern Ireland 1995 to 1997, where her famously frank style made her an instant talking point both sides of the border, despite her sudden arrival from obscurity. Mowlam's courage in defying a brain tumour operation while in office earned her as many friends as enemies. She made friends with many in the republican ranks. Her enemies were mainly in the loyalist camp, in particular Ian Paisley's DUP; she was on record as telling the Reverend to 'eff off' literally at the talks, where US envoy George Mitchell was a fixture. The departure of Ms Mowlam was controversial, and became more so when followed by Peter Mandelson, but the Good Friday Agreement of 10 April 1998 was the eventual happy ending. There was a less happy outcome for Mowlam, whose brain-tumour operation was the indirect cause of her eventual death on 29 August 2005.

P 201 Light My Fire, *Hot Press* 21 January 1999
The Republic of Ireland became the first country in the world to ban smoking in all enclosed work places, including bars and restaurants, on 29 March 2004.

P 208 Fair Shares, *Hot* Press 8 July 1999
After the Telecom Eireann flotation was described as a 'good bet' for all Irish investors, the share price plunged from €60 to €6 very rapidly, leaving a lot of broken hearts in its wake.

P 211 Haughey's Fall, *Hot Press* 22 July1999
Charles James Haughey was sixth Taoiseach of the Republic of Ireland and served three terms, supported by a fiercely devoted following rooted in his North Dublin constituency, where he lived at his Kinsealy estate in considerable style. His 1969 eviction from the Jack Lynch Cabinet followed the 'Arms Scandal,' when Haughey and Neil Blaney were accused of using money earmarked for aid to Northerners to import arms for the Republican movement. Once praised for his 'sex appeal' by Nell in a 1972 *ard fheis* report for *The Irish Times,* Haughey was credited with transforming the economy in the late eighties, mostly by ratcheting the tax rate. But this did not stem emigration; not until the

nineties did the 'Celtic Tiger' roar and exiles come home. Meanwhile, continuing disclosures of shady dealings and corruption in the press weakened his once-impregnable popularity, as did the book of revelations by his mistress Terry Keane. Haughey escaped final retribution in the courts when diagnosed with prostate cancer, a condition that subsequently improved.

P 217 Underneath the Cloth, *Hot Press* 25 November 1999
'John Charles McQuaid, Ruler of Catholic Ireland' (O'Brien Press, 1999) by John Cooney, former *Irish Times* religious affairs and Brussels correspondent, alleged that the man who was Ireland's archbishop from 1940 to 1972 had been both homosexual and paedophile. In an unpublished article by the doctor and politician Noel Browne, he was accused of making advances to a young boy by a schools inspector. It was untouchably controversial at the time yet became one of a tsunami of accusations against the clergy that eroded regular Mass attendance from 68 percent to 48 percent in the last decade of the twentieth century.

P 220 Such Lovely People, *Sunday Tribune* 15 August 2000
Tiny Clogheen was at first reported to be unwelcoming to refugees but the Tipperary townlet has since become famed as the opposite. From emigration to immigration overnight was a by-product of Ireland's sudden new hi-tech prosperity that appeared to take the 3.6 million Irish by surprise. For Africans seeking political asylum and Chinese students seeking educations and Eastern Europeans who are economic refugees much as Irish emigrants to America and England used to be, Ireland is a comparatively safe haven. By 2000 one thousand applications per month for asylum came in, according to Ireland's Justice Department. Between 1990 and 2000 some 30,000 asylum applications were filed; long waits and overworked social workers resulted. The country has increased its asylum workforce to 600, and officials say they hope that the average wait time will soon be down to six months.

P 224 Inis Mór, *Suday Tribune* 1 June 2001
The three main Aran Island raise their backs to the Atlantic Ocean from Galway Bay. Iniseer is within rowing distance of the cliffs of Moher in Clare, with 350 souls. Inismaan boasts a museum and a cooperative and about four hundred inhabitants. With its airport and telephone service and electricity installed in the seventies, the third and largest is Inis Mór, in fact not all that big at twelve kilometers by three at its widest point. Once ravaged by emigration, the island that survived the Famine and economic hardship now boasts a growing population of over a thousand. The sheer cliffs of Dun Aenghus are a continuing puzzle for geologists and archaeologists like Westropp and Praeger. They rise as much as three hundred feet from the sea surface, but the sea has eaten away the limestone cliffs at water level and created a vast, jutting outcrop. Waves crash upwards of two hundred feet or more.

P 228 Lily, from *Nell,* paperback edition 2005 (by kind permission of Penguin Books).

INDEX

∞ ∞ ∞ ∞ ∞ ∞ ∞ ∞ ∞ ∞ ∞ ∞ ∞ ∞ ∞ ∞ ∞ ∞ ∞ ∞